*Dear John,
I hope the... weekly, and lif[e]... [e]asier

All my best,
Mike Woodard*

LIONS WERE BORN TO ROAR

A Man's Guide to Tackling Life and Relationships

By Philip K. Hardin, M.A., M.Div.

Copyright © 2011 by Philip K. Hardin

Lions Were Born To Roar:
A Man's Guide to Tackling Life and Relationships
by Philip K. Hardin, M.A., M.Div.

Printed in the United States of America

ISBN 9781613792421

All rights reserved solely by the author. The author guarantees all contents are original and do not infringe upon the legal rights of any other person or work. No part of this book may be reproduced in any form without the permission of the author. The views expressed in this book are not necessarily those of the publisher. Layout by Stacie Schneeflock.

Unless otherwise indicated, Bible quotations are taken from The New American Standard Bible®. Copyright © 1960, 1962, 1963, 1968, 1971, 1972, 1973, 1975, 1977, 1995 by The Lockman Foundation. Used by permission. All rights reserved.

www.xulonpress.com

To my friend and brother, Dr. Dennis L. Gilbert.

I miss you, Bro!

And

To all the men who have shared their story

at the Men's Coaching Weekends.

"The journey to wholeness for a man starts with a reality check. Phil's book does an excellent job of showing a man his reality and as a result, is a stimulus for real and lasting changes. This is a journey that Phil is well acquainted with both personally and professionally as he helps many move forward."
— Billy Mink, MD, Associate Professor of Pediatrics

"The gift of Phil's book reached me with God's perfect timing. It helped me take an honest look at myself -- my strengths, my joys … alongside of the dark, confusing, and empty areas of my heart. I have found a new passion to become a better father, a better husband, a better mentor to other men, a better friend."
— Jeff Cook – C Spire Wireless, Senior Product Manager

"As a minister I am well acquainted with men's life struggles, family issues, addictions, and family dysfunction that they deal with but don't talk about. The concepts in Phil's book have changed me, and changed the way I approach other men."
— Mike McCool, Minister of Church Education

"Phil Hardin writes not from a theoretical perspective but from the laboratory experiment born in the fire of his own personal journey and decades of effective counseling and men's ministry. I have spent years working in men's ministry and recovery programs and Phil's unique approach to helping men is the most effective I've seen."
— Roane Hunter, President, Life Coaching Systems, Inc.

"My wife and I both agree that the lessons of this book have helped me to grow more in the last year than in any other time in our marriage. These principles truly help me be a better educator who now can teach and lead like a Lion."
— Jeff Anderton, Academic Dean, The Veritas School

"The biblical concepts within these pages helped me find a road map for healing and has given me real hope. Lions Were Born to Roar will change culture — one man at a time."
— Jorge Liceaga, Veterans Service Representative

CONTENTS

PROLOGUE: Who Am I? 3

INTRODUCTION: Why Read This Book? 8

CHAPTER ONE: The Bull 13

CHAPTER TWO: The Chameleon 33

CHAPTER THREE: The Turtle 54

CHAPTER FOUR: The Lion 75

EPILOGUE: Remember This 112

Acknowledgments

Many of the men who are most responsible for the content of this book must remain anonymous. I have learned so much from the men who have courageously shared their broken stories in order to pursue healing through the acceptance of other men. They have taught me to love, how to be honest, and how to genuinely care for another man. I am humbled to call "friend" the many brave men who have overcome guilt, shame, and fear to move into the community of others who offer so much to one another. I am honored and proud to have sat in their presence.

I especially am grateful for the close friends and mentors who have offered brotherhood to me. I am especially grateful for my friend, the late Denny Gilbert, who became such a brother to me in my greatest time of need. I am grateful for friends like Phil Dixon, Charles Waterloo, Richard Ridgway, Dr. Billy Mink, John Musselman, Ron Mumbower, Roane Hunter, Jorge Liceaga, and Larry Brown who have been special to me as we have shared openly and honestly in the "good and bad" of life. To all the men who are too numerous to mention that are part of my life that allow me to see Jesus in their vulnerability and courage. I am a blessed man to have so many brothers.

I am grateful for the many who have read the manuscript and offered helpful feedback. Thank you to Barbara Wicks, Dianne Balch, Bill Taylor, Carla Dearman, John Zehr, and Jeannie Williford. Thanks to Lacy Madden for adding her artistic talents to the effort. Sean Fowlds offered professional feedback that added the final shine to the manuscript. To Lynn Davis, my Administrative Assistant, I am appreciative of her attention to details that frees me to do what I love.

Many people sustained me in this project, yet my dear wife Karla, is foremost of all. Without her encouragement and wise counsel, I would never be the man I am. She is by best friend, passionate companion, and the one I love exploring life with. And to my daughters, Audrey and Abigail, I give thanks for making me a proud father and being patient with me when I am preoccupied with my own interests. Girls, you are my joy!

PSALM 16:11

Thou wilt make known to me the path of life;
In Thy presence is fullness of joy;
In Thy right hand there are pleasures forever.
New American Standard

Now you've got my feet on the life path,
All radiant from the shining of your face.
Ever since you took my hand,
I'm on the right way.
The Message

You will show me the way of life,
Granting me the joy of your presence
And the pleasures of living with you forever.
New Living Translation

You make known to me the path of life;
in your presence there is fullness of joy;
at your right hand are pleasures forevermore.
English Standard Version

You will show me the path of life;
In Your presence is fullness of joy;
At Your right hand are pleasures forevermore.
New King James Version

PROLOGUE: Who Am I?

I write to paint myself.
French Philosopher Michel de Montaigne

A thief is only there to steal and kill and destroy.
I came so they can have real and eternal life,
more and better life than they ever dreamed of.
John 10:10 (The Message)

I was deeply depressed. I felt lost. I was hopelessly disconnected from my family. I felt empty and numb on the inside. I walked around in a shell. People liked me and I liked people. But I felt hollow, like a man with no heart. I felt like a fake who was living a lie. I was tired. And I felt very guilty and all alone.

This is how I described myself several years ago. I was a husband with a great wife and two beautiful daughters. I had so much going for me on the outside, but on the inside I felt dead. Life was not working even though, to others, everything appeared positive and promising.

I was living life in a state of emotional paralysis. However, I thought I was really in touch with myself because I felt such empathy for others. I could share their pain and their joys. I could go to movies and cry over the sad parts. I was so confused by the fact that I felt so bound to others, yet I couldn't connect with myself. Being unable to reconcile such a split inside of myself was killing me. My life was a contradiction.

I had just celebrated my 37th birthday. I was working with an internationally known organization committed to building leaders. I was also working with the business and professional community in Philadelphia as a counselor, mentor, and trainer. I loved God, believed that Jesus had saved me from my sins, and I attended church. I was well-respected and reasonably competent, but I was missing something.

I was experiencing what many would describe as a mid-life crisis. I could not point to any particular thing that was wrong with my life, yet nothing in me seemed satisfying. I remember sitting with a friend and describing how dead I felt: "I feel so hopeless. I don't know what to do. I seem to be able to help everyone but myself. I am depressed, lonely, and tired. I want to die."

He was bewildered. He wanted to help me, but he could not penetrate my cold, dead heart. I felt more hopeless and helpless than I had ever felt. The only way of escaping the pain seemed to be to take my own life. Thankfully, I knew that was not the answer, though in my darkest moments I understood how people could consider such an option!

I blamed Karla, my wife, for not giving more of herself. Even though she was the mother of two baby girls, I expected her to be better at caring for my needs. I was not aware of how angry I was at her and everyone else on whom I had placed the responsibility of making me feel valued and fulfilled. I was unaware of the resentment I felt for the emptiness I was feeling. I felt like a victim, and I acted like a victim.

My wife had a third "baby" on her hands, and I was blind to how destructive I was to my own life and the life of our family. For months, maybe even years, I had been running and running … trying to discover what was missing…and yet had never realized that's what I was doing.

I often thought about just driving away. I was working in Dallas, and I would lay awake in my bed imagining where I would go. If I drove west, I could be in Albuquerque. I had driven through there once, and had found it different and beautiful in a way that I had never seen. Or, I could drive north and be in Wyoming or Montana. I had once hiked to the top of Medicine Bow Peak and could see the top of Long's Peak in Colorado. I wanted something different, something that would help me feel alive. My life did not make sense.

As I had often done in the past, I went to a private place away from my home for meditation and reflection in hopes of getting my head on straight. I was there, talking on the phone with Karla when she suggested that I read *When Your World Makes No Sense* by Dr. Henry Cloud. (The book has since been retitled *Changes That Heal*). I knew I needed something so I went to a bookstore, and of course, they didn't have it in stock. So I had it shipped overnight. I think I paid more for the shipping than the cost of the book. I read it in one day. This book gave me a glimmer of hope that just maybe someone could help me find myself.

I had gone on my retreat feeling hopeless, but I was open to trying something else. When I arrived home, I found that my wife was committed to seeing me face my demons. She told me I had been offered a place at Dr. Cloud's facility where I could begin a deliberate growing process. Assuming I was willing, I could work directly with Dr. Cloud and his team in California. I was willing! Two days later, I flew to Los Angeles. I had hoped, even in my numbed-out state, that I could find life.

I assumed that the setting would be some sort of retreat-like facility with a lake, ducks to feed, and benches on which to sit and contemplate my life. When I arrived at the clinic, I discovered it to be a wing in a small, cinderblock community hospital in a suburb of Los Angeles. No ducks! No lake! No benches! I entered the hospital and was promptly fitted with the customary orange, plastic wristband that is standard issue for any mental health facility. That is when I began to think that this was really serious; this was no retreat, and I was screwed. I wanted to start running again.

I was immediately introduced to my counselor, Dan (I was arrogantly expecting Dr. Cloud there to welcome me). Dan sat across from me and began asking me questions that I tried to answer in a way that would help him know just how depressed I was. After about 20 minutes of this kind of conversation, Dan said to me, "You are really angry." I remember thinking, "What an idiotic statement. I am depressed, and if this counselor keeps thinking I am angry, I am going to beat the crap out of him. Angry? I am not angry, stupid. I AM DEPRESSED!" Even though I was thinking these thoughts, I did not respond. I stared blankly into Dan's face, feeling lost and confused.

I eventually did meet Dr. Cloud and the rest of the team. I spent 30 days working through my life story. I was in a place where a group of well-trained people "kicked my emotional butt" in the most loving and direct way imaginable. I heard the stories of many other hurting and confused professionals in their 30s and 40s who were as lost as I was. Most of them loved God, had good families, and were seeking to grow their careers, yet they could not seem to connect to themselves, to others, or to life in a satisfying way.

I began telling my story, just being open and honest about my life. As I did, counselors offered skilled assessment and feedback. Fellow patients offered their experience of sitting with me and hearing my story. They were neither critical nor judgmental about how I handled my "great life" so ungratefully. Together, counselors and patients formed a safe, relational circle around me. They were committed to offering the acceptance and the structure I needed to find my real self.

I was being pushed to confront areas of my life, some of which I was unaware of and others issues I was hiding. I had covered these areas through an intense compulsion to help others and work hard. The fatal error I had made was not being open and honest about my own pain. I had deliberately tried to live as if I could find healing without acknowledging what was going on inside my skin.

I was also unaware of how distant and how self-absorbed I was in relating to my wife. She is not one to complain, but when she did offer her experience of me, I discounted her words because I did not experience ME that way! I would think, "how could that be true when MY experience of ME is so different?" My own view was more important than her thoughts and feedback. That response worked fine when my view was accurate, but it was a fatal strategy when I was blind to how I related to my wife and how that made her feel disregarded by me.

At the end of 30 days of deliberate commitment to growth, I returned to the Philadelphia airport where Karla and our two babies greeted me and welcomed me home. Now it was time to take what I had learned at the clinic and integrate it into the real world. I was scared, excited, and humbled. A team of professionals had helped me identify my life issues and the defenses that were preventing me from connecting to myself and others. I had worked in a way that gave me insight, equipped me with new skills, taught me to value my feelings, and showed me how to live in community — all as a means of understanding how life really works.

I was in a new place. I wanted to know how to be a man and how to connect to those I loved. I wanted to be the man God designed me to be. I wanted to be a husband who could love his wife and feel connected to her. As a dad, I wanted to offer myself to my children in such a way that would allow them to experience my presence in a loving and accepting way. I wanted to have friends with whom I was really connected. I wanted to know them and for them to know me. I wanted to know how to live!

This book is my story and a collection of other men's stories that I have been privileged to hear from them. I offer it as a way of helping you tell your story and, in doing so, to find your life. I invite you to discover how life really works! I invite you to be a man and, in the words of the apostle Paul, "act like men."

> Be on the alert, stand firm in the faith,
> Act like men, be strong.
> *1 Corinthians 16:13*

INTRODUCTION: Why Read This Book?

I have spent thousands of hours sitting with men who are competent, capable, and gifted, yet they often share a similar sadness about their lives. They are perplexed as to how to make their life work and they often express their frustration by blaming and criticizing their loved ones. Most men have few, if any meaningful friendships. Many are depressed and lonely because they do not know how to connect with their wives and children. I hear them saying, "I wish I knew. I wish I knew what she wants from me. I wish I knew how to connect with my children. I wish I knew how to get my family in a better place. I wish I knew how I could make life work."

I believe reading this book will be like sitting in a counseling session without going to a counselor's office. The concepts introduced here will challenge you to think about your life in a different way. They will help you begin the process of acknowledging your areas of brokenness and allow you to form a solid foundation for life as it was meant to be.

God offers LIFE and He has provided the resources through His Son, Jesus Christ. And though He offers it freely, He requires us to walk with Him in a journey of discovery and to acknowledge our weakness and failures as a means of becoming whole. You were designed to receive and experience love, to openly share yourself with God and others, and to live in a deep bond of trust with Him and others as you face the challenges of life. Scripture invites you to see the healing God has offered to you. Listen to His call:

> What a God we have!
> And how fortunate we are to have him,
> This Father of our Master Jesus!
> Because Jesus was raised from the dead,
> We've been given a brand-new life and have everything
> to live for, Including a future in heaven—
> And the future starts now!
> God is keeping careful watch over us and the future.
> The Day is coming when you'll have it all—life healed and whole.
> *1 Peter 1:3-5 (The Message)*

WOW! Is that really possible ... a new life ... a better future ...

healing from old hurts and wounds…wholeness…life as God designed? YES, it is possible! I am experiencing it and I have seen countless other men find the life God has promised.

Throughout these chapters, you will be exposed to two important concepts: Being Known and Living in Community. You were designed to know and to be known. You were made to live in community—in a family, in a marriage, to have friends, to have support, to live together with others. For you to experience the life for which you were designed, it is critical that you understand the concepts of Being Known and Living in Community.

This book will guide you through four metaphors against which you can measure your life. A man is like a Lion, a Bull, a Chameleon, and a Turtle. To become like a Lion is to reach the place of maturity and fulfillment. The Bull, Chameleon, and Turtle are characterized by maladaptive behaviors men develop for coping and survival. Every man will have some aspects of the Bull, Chameleon, and Turtle living in him. However, the more he is willing to be like a Lion, the more he will become the man he was designed to be. Ultimately, being like a Lion is to be like Christ, who is the Lion.

> There was no one—no one in Heaven,
> No one on earth, no one from the underworld
> —able to break open the scroll and read it.
> I wept and wept that no one was found able to open
> the scroll,
> Able to read it.
> One of the Elders said,
> "Don't weep.
> Look—the Lion from Tribe Judah,
> The Root of David's Tree, has conquered.
> He can open the scroll, can rip through the
> seven seals."
> *Revelation 5:3-5 (The Message)*

Lion: As a Lion, a man demonstrates the courage to know himself and allow others to know him.

Bull: As a Bull, a man is blind to parts of himself that are obvious to others.

Chameleon: As a Chameleon, a man fears sharing the parts of

himself that he knows about but doesn't want to reveal to others.

Turtle: As a Turtle, a man lives in a shell of self-protection and is therefore unaware of large parts of himself and others.

Understanding how each of these metaphors applies to your life will help you begin to break old, destructive patterns that prevent you from being known and living in community.

As you consider this model, see Diagram One, which is a form of the Johari Model that illustrates how you were designed and how you have adapted to life. Knowing and being known is essential to living life the way God designed it. When being known is unavailable or the knowing is painful, you adapt in some way to protect yourself and survive. You must know your Self and you must live in Group.

A Community is developed when people know Self and are in a Group. A man who knows Self is a man who has experienced living in a healthy group of family or friends who have supplied lots of acceptance, validation, understanding, direction, and support. When those supplies are available a man develops a true sense of Self and his true heart is nurtured without the shame and guilt that causes survival strategies to develop as false forms of protection. The man who knows Self and is known by the Group is a man who lives in Community.

Quadrant one describes a large area of being known by self and by others. It is the quadrant where life works best. This Quadrant is designed to be the optimum default point. When you are committed to having Quadrant One as your objective, life works. Both good times and times of suffering have meaning and purpose. In this quadrant lives the Lion. Courage is required.

Quadrants Two, Three, and Four are maladaptive strategies people sometimes use to survive the lack of being known in a nurturing, healing way. These are positions and styles of defense that you use to protect yourself from further pain.

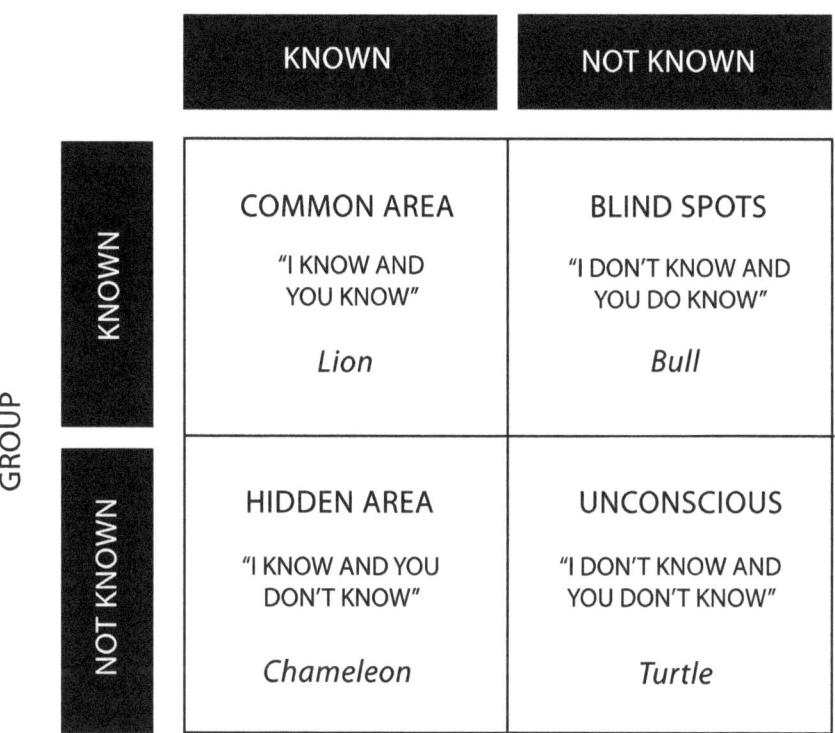

DIAGRAM ONE

As you are guided through the model, you will first be exposed to the three maladaptive quadrants — examining the Bull, the Chameleon, and the Turtle. This will help you to identify what is hindering you from having the life you desire. Then, you will be shown the profile of the Lion and thus be invited into what life can be. You will be able to tackle life and all your relationships with wisdom and skill.

Hundreds of men who have been willing to face their lives through an honest and humble assessment have tested and experienced the concepts in this book. After reading this guide, I hope you will better understand how life works and how God designed you to be. You will be able to reveal yourself to those you love and to receive their love for you. The meaning of life will become clear. You will no longer have to say, "I wish I knew," because you will understand how to connect with and enjoy your wife, family, and friends. You will be able to build something new as Jesus promised:

> Everyone who comes to Me, and hears My words,
> and acts upon them,
> I will show you whom he is like:
> He is like a man building a house, who dug deep
> and laid a foundation upon the rock;
> And when a flood rose, the torrent burst against that
> house and could not shake it,
> Because it had been well built.
> But the one who has heard, and has not acted
> accordingly, is like a man who built a house upon
> the ground without any foundation;
> and the torrent burst against it and immediately it
> collapsed,
> and the ruin of the house was great.
> *Luke 6:47-49*

Welcome to the process. Enjoy your journey. Glad you are here!

CHAPTER ONE
THE BULL

> "It seldom happens that a man changes his life through his habitual reasoning. No matter how fully he may sense the new plans and aims revealed to him by reason, he continues to plod along in old paths until his life becomes frustrating and unbearable — he finally makes the change only when his usual life can no longer be tolerated."
> Leo Tolstoy (Russian Writer 1828-1910)

> "Everyone thinks of changing the world, but no one thinks of changing himself."
> Leo Tolstoy

> But Peter answered and said to Him, "Even though all may fall away because of You, I will never fall away."
> Matthew 26:33

INTRODUCTION

Bryan came to see me by himself. He was in my office because of his wife's insistence. His only problem was his wife. She seemed to be tired of the marriage, and Bryan was deeply disturbed as to what to do about her dissatisfaction. Bryan described Molly as being overly sensitive and too emotional. "She takes everything so seriously. I don't understand why she can't forget about all the little things that seem to get her down and be grateful for the life I have given her." I found Bryan's description of Molly and their marriage to be very revealing. Bryan thought the problem was Molly and so he spoke about Molly's being "grateful for the life I have given her." He did not acknowledge the life they had built together, no mention of shared goals and experiences, no reference of bringing out the best in each other.

I asked Bryan to clarify why he had come to see me. He explained that Molly wanted him to get help and that her counselor suggested that he see a different therapist. I was recommended. I told Bryan I would be glad to assist him in his growth and asked him to tell me more about how he would like to be helped. Bryan continued to describe how Molly seemed to be getting worse and implied that he thought her therapist was not helping matters. "Molly seems to want little to do with me. She is more depressed than I have ever seen her.

She is less able to get on with her life and she sleeps a lot."

Near the end of the session, I said to him, "I cannot help you, Bryan, unless Molly comes with you. I'm not talking about marriage counseling; I just can't help you unless Molly is here." He was confused because Molly had told him she did not want marriage counseling. She wanted Bryan to get help or she could not continue in the marriage. "Bryan," I said, "I need Molly to be here so you can get an accurate picture of YOU. She seems to be telling you things about yourself that you don't see. Therefore, you believe the problem is really about Molly. If you come back to my office without Molly, I believe we will continue to talk about Molly, rather than the real issues that are blocking your ability to have the relationship with her that you want."

Bryan was in a difficult spot. He didn't want to be in counseling to start with and Molly didn't want to be with him anywhere! And now, I was asking him to invite Molly into his therapy. He hated this whole predicament! Reluctantly, he agreed to extend the invitation. (I believe he thought that would at least be a way for me to help Molly and get her away from the other therapist.) In Bryan's mind he felt more in control with my request and left my office ready to GET MOLLY FIXED!

We'll talk more about Molly and Bryan later ….

HOW IS A MAN LIKE A BULL?

A man is like a Bull when he is blind to areas of his life that others see. He thinks he is self-aware. But, in his blindness, he can't see some of the things that are obvious to others.

In Diagram Two, the Bull is a man who has a larger area of Self that is known by Others than the area that is known by him. He is blind to Self. He is unaware of what others experience while connecting with him.

As a Bull, he is typically uninterested in what others think about him or about the problems

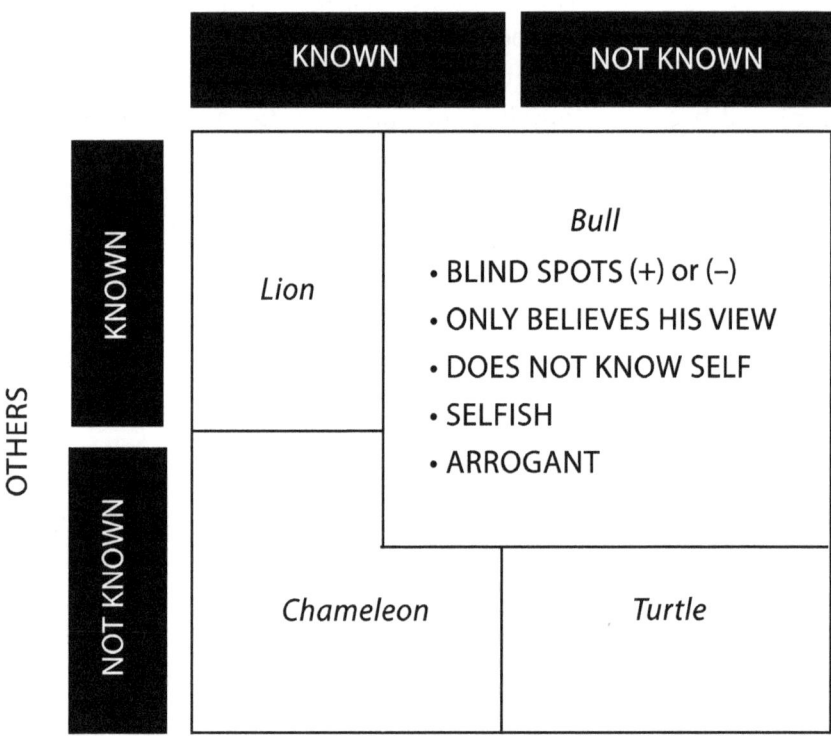

DIAGRAM TWO

others may face while being in partnership with him. His only problem is the uncooperative nature of others. So long as others do what he thinks or believes they should do, then life works. Bryan THINKS life works well if it's working the way he sees it!

A Bull is like a man who snores. He sleeps eight hours and feels rested in the morning. He arrives at the breakfast table to find Mom and the kids tired and sleepy. He cannot figure out why they feel so miserable when he feels so good. He is not aware nor is he interested in how they got to this exhausted place. He laughs when his family explains how he snored so loudly that Mom had to leave their bedroom and even the kids in their own rooms had to place pillows over their heads to protect their eardrums. He has no concept of the window-rattling snores that came from him while he is totally

unconscious of the noise. His whole family is dying because of his behavior, and he is at peace with himself and the world.

A Bull is blind to how he brings discomfort to others. The only discomfort he is interested in is HIS! When others confront him about how they experience him, he is confused at best or he is angry at being falsely accused. In his confusion, he may label others as being "too sensitive" or "too emotional" or even unappreciative of his disciplined, hard-working attempts to provide. In his anger, he may lash back at these "false accusations" in a way that punishes those in his path. He will not tolerate being confronted when he is working so hard at life and his intentions are so pure.

Kirby is another such Bull. He has a great wife and family. They all love him, but he is blind to the parts of him that hurt his wife and children. His wife consistently meets with resistance when she confronts him about his inconsiderate behavior. He typically and predictably moves into his monologue describing how he has worked all his life and how he is working so hard now to provide the lifestyle she now enjoys. He confronts her with what he sees as her ungratefulness or mistakes she has made in their marriage. Kirby is blind to what it is like for his wife and children to be with him.

For Kirby the question, "What is it like for you to be with me?" would seem ridiculous. And yet, if he could go there, it would yield to him the very information that would help him know why his family life is not working. Without a change, though, he would not know what to do with such information. Because he is so entrenched in his views even when he receives the feedback, he is suspicious or discounts it as the foolish perception of his wife or children.

A Bull is blind! How can a blind man see? How can the broken part of a man begin to work? How can a man see what he is so unable to recognize? It seems so pointless to ask a man to see color when he is so blind to anything but black or white. The Bull sees the world his way and no other way. How can anyone ask a man to do something that he cannot do?

The apostle Peter was blind to parts of himself and he needed to know that blindness brought great hurt and pain to him and others, namely Jesus Christ. The words, "I would never …" were painful to hear…painful last words.

> "Even if everyone else falls to pieces on
> account of you, I won't."
> "Don't be so sure," Jesus said.
> "This very night, before the rooster crows up the dawn,
> you will deny me three times."
> Peter protested,
> "Even if I had to die with you,
> I would never deny you."
> All the others said the same thing.
> Matthew 26:33-35 (The Message)

Let's examine some important aspects of the Bull ….

WHAT DOES A BULL WANT?

A Bull wants life to work! He is not interested in feelings or imagination or sensory information. He is so oriented to function that he is dysfunctional. He operates with such a narrow world focus that he is blind to the parts of himself that God intended to work. He sees his perspective as the only meaningful reality.

A Bull will invalidate the one he is with and ignore requests that are irritating or hurtful. He minimizes the discomfort of those around him to the extent that their requests for change go unheeded. The simple fact is that the Bull wants his world to work, but those who don't corporate with him and who try to get him to truly listen to them can become completely frustrated.

When my two daughters were little I enjoyed rolling on the floor with them, throwing them through the air and onto the bed, and tickling them until they were screaming for me to stop. I thought this was great fun that would one day win me my daughters' vote for "Dad of the Year." The problem, however, was my wife's point of view. She feared that somehow the girls would be hurt.

And on those occasions when one would bump her head, fall off the bed, or start crying, my wife would become furious with me. She was heavily influenced by her memory of three uncles who would tickle her mercilessly when she was a little girl. My experience of those playful moments was so different from my wife's. Even to this day, now that the girls are young women, my wife and I cannot talk about those activities and come close to seeing them in a similar light.

In this context, I have been a Bull. I have resented my wife at times for ruining good play times with our girls. I did not want to hear her or validate her feelings about such innocent behaviors. She was "way too sensitive," "too tied to her uncles' treatment of her," and "unaware how careful I was being." Even though I wanted my girls to be validated in their femininity, I did not want them to be fragile or too delicate. I believed this type of play helped them to develop well.

It is possible that all of my beliefs about how I conducted play with my daughters are valid. They certainly have developed well and I am proud of them today. But, the point is how I listened to my wife. As I was entrenched in my viewpoint, unwilling to hear her concerns, and seeing her position as ridiculous, both of us would behave in a deceptive power struggle against one another in order to validate our respective positions.

I did not want to hear that my tickling the girls was unpleasant or harmful to them. I believed I was simply being playful and was tuned out to any discomfort I may have been creating. My wife saw my actions very differently. She believed I ignored my daughters' repeated pleas to stop. To her, I was rough, callous, and totally uninterested in my daughters' feelings.

I could share hundreds of stories, some more severe, to demonstrate what a Bull wants. My personal story simply illustrates how life can be so frustrating for the Bull. One could debate the degree to which my wife projected her childhood tickling experience onto our daughters or the value of a father's masculine play to the healthy

development of daughters, yet that misses the main point. A Bull does not see or respect anyone else's point of view.

The Bull wants others to see life as he does because he is sure his intentions are good, certain that the outcome of his behavior will be positive, and convinced that others are foolish in their positions. The Bull knows that life will work if others will simply cooperate and accept his position. The Bull wants conformity, not diversity. He is committed to his plan and desires for it to be accepted and executed.

The apostle Peter reflects such a position in his blindness. Jesus had a desire to work deeper into the core of Peter's heart by revealing to Peter parts of himself to which he was blind. Consider again the words of Jesus:

> Jesus said to him,
> "Truly I say to you that this very night before a cock crows,
> You shall deny Me three times."
> Peter said to Him,
> "Even if I have to die with You,
> I will not deny You."
> Matthew 26:34-35

OUCH!!!

You know what happened. Peter found out the hard way how blind he was to the parts of himself that were sabotaging the life God intended for him.

A Bull wants his way! He has no value for another person's view of him or the needs of another.

WHAT DOES A BULL FEAR?

I laugh when I think about what a Bull fears. A Bull would never consider such a question. Fear! How can he fear something he does not see, does not believe is relevant, or has never experienced? Fear is not a conscious reality to the Bull, but he is easily threatened and adverse to vulnerability. Only pain speaks to a Bull.

Bull = unconscious or in denial about his fear!

So, how does fear work for the Bull? He is unconscious of his fear at best, and at worst, in complete denial. A Bull will not engage in an open admission about his fear. He is not aware of how much of his behavior in relationships is due to fear of not being in control.

Therefore, the Bull will never change unless he experiences pain. One who is truly blind as to how he operates in the world and how others experience him, will come to his senses only when he loses all hope that his plan will be implemented. Getting the attention of a Bull can be scary. Unless the Bull is in some sort of uncomfortable place, he will not come to his senses. He will remain blind. One must face the Bull like the matador who, wearing red cape and regalia, stares into the eyes of a real bull that could crush him at any moment.

Dan is another Bull who could not see how his behavior had resulted in severe problems for his wife. For years, Lisa had complained about Dan's business practices, his relationship with their children, and his addiction to alcohol. Dan heard Lisa's request for change as complaint and criticism. She was never satisfied. He doubted if their marriage would last because Lisa was so uncooperative and unfulfilled. Dan's only pain was that Lisa wasn't getting with the program.

Dan failed to see that his business practices had resulted in thousands of dollars of debt. He always believed the next deal would cure his family's problems. Discussions with Lisa about finances resulted in fight after fight. He believed Lisa was unrealistic in her treatment of him and his business plan. Whenever they sat and talked his resentment grew because Lisa's argument never matched his. He had a logical view of how they got to where they were and a logical plan for how he was going to get them to a better place. Dan felt superior to Lisa in the areas of business and finance. He believed she simply needed to take good care of the children and spend less money. He was frustrated with her lack of business and financial savvy and angry because she resisted doing exactly what he wanted her to do.

Dan resented Lisa's repeated observations about how he related to the children. He was confused because in his mind, she was critical of him either for being too involved or being distant. She never seemed to be satisfied with his approach to being a dad. From his point of view, their parenting did not work because Lisa expected too much. Dan believed if Lisa would keep the house clean and be a better disciplinarian, he could get some rest when he was at home, instead of being consumed by the chaos she allowed in the home. He wanted Lisa to get off his back about the children. He hated the pain of being so unappreciated.

In order to get some relief from business stress and life in general, Dan increased his drinking. Lisa noticed that he drank more when he traveled. He used business trips as opportunities to indulge in temporary comfort through "a few drinks with the guys." Predictably, he was indignant when Lisa confronted him about his drinking. He had enough pressure on him without Lisa's overly sensitive nature. Dan was in pain, and he wanted some relief.

By the time Lisa came to me asking for help, she was desperate and exhausted. After hearing her story, I did my best to give Lisa hope. I looked directly at her and said, "Lisa, you are a brave woman to have supported Dan as you have. But, if you want Dan to get better, you will have to confront him in such a way that he will experience pain. I am not talking about nagging, threats, or manipulation. What I am talking about is clear, direct statements of what is going on WITH YOU, what YOU need from Dan, and the consequences if changes are not made." Listening to my words, Lisa seemed frightened and at the same time hopeful. Her response was remarkable.

Lisa was far more courageous and wise than I had first perceived her to be. She actually called her pastor, two of Dan's friends, her parents, and Dan's brother. She organized an intervention by gathering all these people in a friend's home and inviting Dan to come by the friend's home for a neighborhood planning meeting. When Dan entered he was confronted by his family and friends. Lisa let Dan know that she could no longer go on as she had. She told him he must choose either to go to a treatment center for his alcohol abuse or leave their home.

Dan was now squarely faced with pain of his own making: the kind of pain that required him to acknowledge that his actions did hurt others in his world and that they were no longer willing to bear it. As long as Dan could pin the tail on someone else's donkey, he would. Pain can be a great variable in healing if the pain is more than just "being frustrated with how things are not working for me." Purposeful pain is discomfort that actually invites a deeper relationship with another as a result of change. Lisa was offering Dan something new while clearly communicating what was not acceptable.

All true healing is relational. For healing to take place, relationships must be repaired. Life is not so much about fixing problems as it is about healing relationships. The Bull is really not interested in someone else's pain. He is interested only in his pain. He must face the fear of losing the relationships that make HIS WORLD work. He must be brought face-to-face with the reality that someone else exists in the world and is not afraid to confront him. To be in a relationship with a Bull requires that you not be intimidated by his control or pity him in his sulking. You must invite him to take responsibility for his behavior that is bringing destruction to the relationship.

Seeing a Bull move into a place of fear—LOSING HIS WORLD—is an amazing moment to behold. Miracles occur when Bulls become aware of blind spots. Scales drop from their eyes, and they see for the first time. On the other hand, I have seen Bulls become even more hardened and willful when confronted. They can become angry and resentful when their world is attacked. In that case, you must walk away from the Bull and not engage in his control or manipulation that keeps him in the continued place of blindness. You must allow him to suffer the consequences of his behavior. In reality,

even when confronted with the fact that their world is not working, some Bulls will not change.

Consider Peter when he really saw what Jesus had been telling him.

> And a little later the bystander came up and said to Peter,
> "Surely you too are one of them;
> For the way you talk gives you away."
> Then he began to curse and swear,
> "I do not know the man!"
> And immediately a cock crowed.
> And Peter remembered the word which Jesus had said,
> "Before a cock crows, you will deny Me three times."
> And he went out and wept bitterly.
> Matthew 26:73-75

Peter experienced pain as he saw his blindness. He felt sorrow and he was a changed man. He had heard the voice of another, i.e. Jesus, in the depths of his heart and after he repented he experienced the contrition, the sorrow, and the humility that allowed him to become a great spokesman for the kingdom of God. In contrast, consider Judas.

> Then when Judas, who had betrayed Him,
> Saw that He had been condemned,
> He felt remorse and returned the thirty pieces of silver to the chief priests and elders,
> Saying, "I have sinned by betraying innocent blood."
> But they said,
> "What is that to us? See to that yourself!"
> And he threw the pieces of silver into the sanctuary and departed;
> And he went away and hanged himself.
> Matthew 27:3-5

Judas realized what he had done. Though Scripture indicates he felt remorse, there is no indication that he changed. Feeling bad that your way is not working is very different from accepting responsibility for your actions and walking in new ways. Change is possible, and restoration a promise, but it is not easy. Courage is required!

Redemptive pain empowers us to recover or restore that which has been lost. It reveals to us how our behavior affects our loved ones. It helps us understand and accept that we can lose the ones we love if we do not allow their view to be a valued part of our reality. Having reached this level of awareness, it gives us the incentive to make the changes necessary to repair the relationships we treasure.

A Bull who faces his fear can do that! And that's NO BULL!

WHAT IS IT LIKE TO BE WITH A BULL?

Living with a Bull is like talking to someone and eventually realizing the person has not been listening and has very little interest in having you repeat what you just said. It is like giving a special gift to someone who seems almost annoyed that you took the time to engage in such nonsense. The Bull is not interested in how you experience him.

To live with a Bull is to experience "validation deprivation."

You will not be affirmed in your thinking about life. The only way a Bull appreciates you is when you simply do what he wants you to do. Even then you do not get validation, but simply a look that says, "Now you got it right … what's for dinner?" Living with a Bull can drain you of self-worth and well-being. The Bull is blind to how you experience him.

The Bull is neither a humble person, nor is he maliciously proud. He is just so unaware of how he affects others that he can be incredibly narcissistic, selfish, and arrogant. Humility comes from our ability to count ourselves as less important than another and a willingness to be in tune with another's experience of the world. The Bull is tuned in to one station … HIS

OWN! He does not hear the voice of others. He is sometimes wrong, but never in doubt.

John and Barbara came to see me through the recommendations of a mutual friend. I observed as they came into my office. John entered first and seemed to choose his place deliberately and then nodded to Barbara as if to indicate where she should sit. John was a large man, appeared to be in good shape, and was well dressed. Barbara was attractive and polite, but seemed to have little energy or presence in the room. As I asked them how I could be of help, John quickly shared his perception of the problem and described what Barbara needed to do to fix their marriage.

He saw Barbara as weak, uninteresting, and unwilling to do what he had repeatedly asked her to do. She was unwilling to do what would help him think better of her. Each time he spoke, John seemed to take away another piece of whatever life remained in Barbara. She would defend herself, but I could imagine what she must be feeling. Speaking in John's shadow seemed to cause her words to bounce off the walls like tennis balls off a backboard.

The more I listened to John and Barbara, the more I found myself disliking John. His arrogance was toxic. I was feeling sick, and I wondered just how accustomed Barbara was to this kind of poison. If I was feeling the effects of John so quickly, I could only imagine what Barbara must have already endured. She had lived in this destructive state for so long that she truly was confused about how much of what John was saying was right. She was overpowered and over-matched by John.

John had no interest in really understanding what was going on with Barbara or with him. He knew what he needed for his well-being and he was in my office only to help me help Barbara. And he fully expected me to implement his plan. He had no real desire to hear what I thought would really help him and Barbara find a deeper intimacy and satisfaction in their marriage.

At this point in their relationship, Barbara was so depleted of any sense of who she was that she could not have expressed herself well even if John had been willing to listen. The most Barbara could do was to somehow disagree with how John framed her and their marriage. She would protest his explanation, but mostly from a sense of self-preservation, not a strong, assertive voice letting him know who she was. When John spoke to Barbara he communicated such displeasure about her that watching him in action was like watching an angry wolf rip the heart from an innocent, much smaller animal. He was relentless; she was defenseless.

Because a Bull is unaware of how he hurts and ignores others, he is generally clueless and uninterested in how others view and experience him. He is intentional about the direction in which he is moving and will often run over others if they stay in his path. When dancing with a Bull, expect to have your toes stepped on, then as you are hobbling to a chair, don't be surprised to hear him say, "Why are you not dancing anymore?"

HOW CAN A BULL CHANGE?

The Bull can change only when he humbles himself enough to solicit feedback about how others experience him. The Bull who is willing to change begins to ask: "What's it like for you to be with me?" or "What is your experience of me in this circumstance?" Healing begins when he moves away from being self centered and being self important. He must give up life as he knows it in order to connect with another. When a Bull drinks from the cup of humility, he is transformed as he begins to value someone else's reality and experience over his own. Change for a Bull is reduced to this formula: another's experience is greater than my experience.

For the Bull, this journey is a near-death experience. He will most likely feel death in the form of fear and anger. He will feel overtaken and engulfed by the ones he is struggling to know. He will fight against this like a man caught in a whirlpool, struggling to regain

control and afraid of drowning in unknown water. Anger and the need to control will speak to him and offer him the power he needs to rescue himself from death. To begin the healing process, the Bull must resist these false securities and allow himself to embrace another's reality. He must die to the concept that his is the only reality. The Bull must humbly offer himself to the process of receiving from another. He must be willing to be led, if even by a little child, i.e. a less experienced person. He will find this place to be VERY SCARY!

At the beginning of this chapter, I introduced you to Bryan and Molly. When Bryan came to see me, he was the typical Bull. He was blind to the weak and broken parts of his life. Molly had survived their marriage, but was now unwilling and unable to continue. Her sense of self and her own reality were being swallowed by Bryan's overpowering nature and his blindness to the way he was hurting Molly.

As I had requested, Bryan invited Molly to join him in my office. I learned a long time ago that trying to do individual therapy with a Bull is foolish. When a Bull sees only his reality, he has neither the ability nor the incentive to alter behavior which he perceives as being right. In individual therapy, a Bull will consistently blame and criticize someone else for his circumstance.

Sitting in my office with Molly at his side, Bryan began the painful and scary process of listening to Molly's reality. Watching Bryan humbly but awkwardly begin to give value to Molly's reality was both humorous and pleasing. Bryan was entering a place that was totally foreign to him. He was exploring the unknown areas of Molly. He trusted me enough to let me help him hear what Molly was saying without feeling like he was going to be forced to give up all of his power and just do it Molly's way. Bryan was receiving feedback about himself, becoming exposed to his blind spots, and learning how to see Molly differently.

Each week that Bryan and Molly came into my office I would invite Bryan to tell me about his week with Molly. I would never ask

Molly to say anything until Bryan had fully shared his viewpoint. When he finished, I would ask Bryan what he thought Molly might have experienced relative to the same circumstance. At first, Bryan would look at me as if to say, "What does it matter? I just told you what happened." As he was forced to acknowledge that such behavior was the reason he was sitting in my office in the first place and would result in his coming back indefinitely, Bryan learned there was something more. He would sheepishly glance at Molly as if bewildered that she might tell a different story.

I leaned toward Bryan and invited him into a dangerous place: "Bryan, ask Molly what she experienced." Inviting a Bull to ask such a question is like asking a non-swimmer if he would like to swim the English Channel. I prepared Bryan for the likelihood that Molly's viewpoint was probably going to be different from his. And that he would most likely find it a challenge to value what Molly was saying. From past experience, I knew that he placed a very low value on Molly's viewpoint. I coached him, "Be careful, Bryan, this might be dangerous for you!" Bryan looked at Molly and reluctantly asked for her perspective. He was willing to consider a reality other than his own. The Bull was beginning to become a LION!

Transformation was happening before my eyes. For Bryan this was equal to a currency exchange. Anytime you travel into a new country, you must exchange your dollar for the currency that is accepted in that country. Bryan was making an emotional currency exchange, exchanging his "emotional dollar" for the currency of Molly. It was a miraculous transaction to watch. It is possible! I have seen it happen.

CONCLUSION

I have sat with many Bulls through the years. These men are blind to the ways they hurt others and are unaware of their own pain. These Bulls have little or no ability to look inside themselves and find the hurt that keeps them locked into highly defended places of fear and anger. They are blind to important aspects of self and to the experience that others have of them.

When a fellow named Charlie came to one of the Men's Coaching Weekends, he was truly hurting. He was recently divorced and as a result separated from his children. He did not understand why his life was not working. It took a routine stop for fast food to open his eyes. While trying to place the order correctly, "Charlie, being Charlie," was astounded to hear his daughter say with complete annoyance, "Dad, why do you always have to try and control everything!" Charlie shared with me and the other men that in that moment he somehow heard the voice of his former wife, his other children, and even some friends corroborating his need for control. He had an epiphany regarding how profoundly his fear and anger affected the lives of the ones he loved the most. The voice of his daughter had penetrated years of defense. At that moment, Charlie got it! He heard the music of another. The Bull had finally heard the call to be different. Charlie wanted to be real!

The Bull in you can be defeated if you will open yourself to the voice of another and allow yourself to be known. You have blind spots that others see in you but you do not see in yourself. Will you place yourself in the humble position to receive? Will you receive the feedback from others, value it enough to understand the way they experience you, and be willing to own any behavior that hurts another? The Bull in you can be defeated by feedback from safe and loving people if you are willing to listen. You must receive!

A safe person is someone you trust that has your best interests at heart. They are NOT trying to take advantage of you, but desire to be closer to you. They care about you and truly want to help you be the person God created you to be. The question for you is: WILL YOU TRUST THEM? You must TRUST!

Two important questions for a Bull to use as tools to bring closeness in relationships and healing from his blindness about himself are:

    1. "What do I do that pushes you away from me?"
    2. "What do I do that draws you toward me?"

A Bull must begin to trust others and ask for their feedback or he will continue to be blind to the parts of himself that he believes are issues with others.

Do you want to be known? Do you want to defeat the Bull? Do you want to be real? Do you want to become a Lion?

You choose!

REMEMBER THIS:

- The Bull is blind.
- The Bull is blind to areas of his life that others see, but he does not see.
- The Bull sees his perspective as the only reality there is or that is meaningful.
- The Bull believes that life will work if others will simply take his position and cooperate.
- The Bull seems to fear nothing. Fear is not part of his reality. His only fear is the possibility of his world not working.
- The Bull must be brought face-to-face with the fear that someone else exists in the world and will confront him.
- The Bull is unaware of how he hurts others, ignores others, and is generally clueless and uninterested in others' views and experiences of him.
- The Bull must be open to feedback and the viewpoint of others.
- The Bull must die to the concept that his is the only reality.
- A Bull can become a Lion by valuing and listening to the feedback from people he trusts.

> Don't put your life in the hands of experts
> who know nothing of life, of salvation life.
> Mere humans don't have what it takes;
> when they die, their projects die with them.
> Instead, get help from the God of Jacob,
> put your hope in God and know real blessing!
> God made sky and soil,
> sea and all the fish in it.
> He always does what he says—
> he defends the wronged,
> he feeds the hungry.

> God frees prisoners—
> he gives sight to the blind,
> he lifts up the fallen.
> GOD loves good people, protects strangers,
> takes the side of orphans and widows,
> but makes short work of the wicked.
>
> Psalm 146:3-9 (The Message)

> God's Message, the God who created the cosmos, stretched out the skies,
> laid out the earth and all that grows from it,
> Who breathes life into earth's people, makes them alive with his own life:
> "I am God. I have called you to live right and well.
> I have taken responsibility for you, kept you safe.
> I have set you among my people to bind them to me,
> and provided you as a lighthouse to the nations,
> To make a start at bringing people into the open, into light:
> opening blind eyes,
> releasing prisoners from dungeons, emptying the dark prisons.
> I am God. That's my name.
> I don't franchise my glory, don't endorse the no-god idols.
> Take note: The earlier predictions of judgment have been fulfilled.
> I'm announcing the new salvation work.
> Before it bursts on the scene, I'm telling you all about it."
>
> Isaiah 42:4-6 (The Message)

CHAPTER TWO
THE CHAMELEON

> "If the secret of being a bore is to tell all,
> the secret of pleasing is to say just enough to be
> —not understood, but divined."
> Remy de Gourmont (French Novelist 1858-1915)

> And do not participate in the unfruitful deeds of darkness,
> But instead expose them;
> For it is disgraceful even to speak of the things
> which are done by them in secret.
> Ephesians 5:11-12

INTRODUCTION

The Chameleon is the man who adapts to life by only offering parts of himself. He knows things about himself that he is unwilling or fearful to share with others. He has a high degree of self-awareness, but keeps in secret much of what would help others to know him. He needs to reveal more of what he knows about himself in order to be known by others. Being known by others is a dilemma and creates tension for the Chameleon. Let me introduce you to a Chameleon...

Larry is one of the most competent men I know. He is talented, likable, and caring. He has the ability to sit with his friends and be genuinely interested in their lives. People who meet Larry see him as someone who truly wants to make a difference in the world. If you sat with Larry, you would like him.

When Larry and Ellen began counseling, Larry had just had an affair. Ellen was devastated. She had given her heart to Larry and he had betrayed her and their marriage vows. They had been married ten years and had three children. Life seemed very good until Larry did the unthinkable. How could he do such a thing? How could he be so wonderful and commit such an hurtful act? Ellen was hurt and confused. Larry seemed frozen, detached, and unemotional.

The more Ellen tried to express her disbelief, the more Larry seemed to become detached. He just wanted the pain to go away. He wanted Ellen to stop bringing up his shameful behavior. He wanted all the chaos to stop.

When Larry finally spoke, all he could do was to make promises that he would never again do anything like that. He did not want to hurt Ellen, and he repeatedly declared how sorry he was for what he had done. Larry seemed to want to deflect the pain rather than accept responsibility for the hurt he had caused. He sat in the guilt and shame of his behavior like a little child caught in a forbidden act, but not as a man who really wanted to be forgiven and reconciled with his wife.

Ellen was confused as to what to do. She loved Larry. She wanted to rebuild the trust and to provide for their three children the family they deserved. However, she could not penetrate the wall that Larry seemed to live behind. He was trying to say the right thing, but his words seemed to be more about protecting himself than about welcoming Ellen into his world. He said little that really helped Ellen feel safe with him.

What was really going on with Larry? What would it take for Larry to rebuild trust with Ellen?

HOW IS A MAN LIKE A CHAMELEON?

We sometimes use the Chameleon as a metaphor to describe humans who are changeable. Chameleons are known for their adaptive ability to change color and blend into their surroundings. It is a common perception that they do this to hide themselves from view. Likewise, a man is like a Chameleon when he purposely hides parts of himself from others because he is afraid they will find him to be unacceptable.

Larry is a typical Chameleon. He does all he can do to keep from being exposed. He is gifted at aligning himself with what another person is feeling or thinking. His ability to join with others allows him to be loved and appreciated by most everyone.

Chameleon = attuned to environment versus self or others

A Chameleon is more attuned to his environment than he is to himself or to the true values of those closest to him. He tends to be anchored in the wishes of others and is, therefore, more responsive to needy people or those who give him lots of attention.

Diagram Three reveals a large hidden area, or private self, that the Chameleon does not share with others. Because he fears rejection, he hides his known failings and deflects attention from himself by focusing on others. He does not realize that hiding and ignoring his brokenness robs others of the opportunity to love him through the healing process. He forfeits the growth of character he would experience if he revealed his true self to those who want to know him intimately.

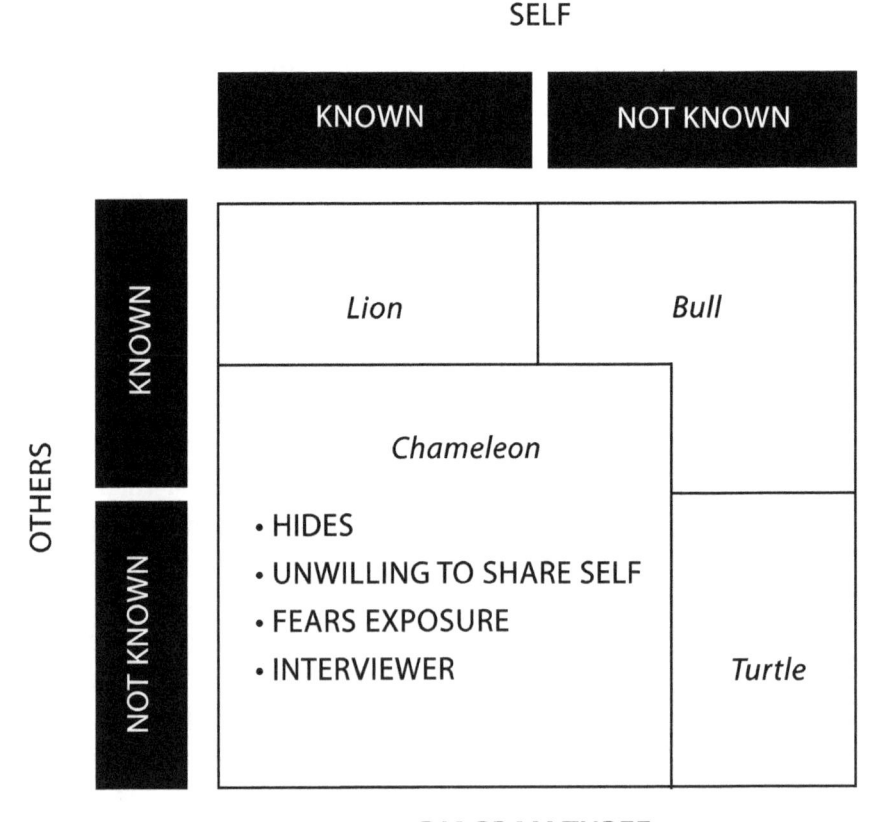

SELF

	KNOWN	NOT KNOWN
OTHERS — KNOWN	Lion	Bull
OTHERS — NOT KNOWN	Chameleon • HIDES • UNWILLING TO SHARE SELF • FEARS EXPOSURE • INTERVIEWER	Turtle

DIAGRAM THREE

When a Chameleon recognizes something about himself that is embarrassing or shameful, he copes by keeping it hidden from others. He makes a vow, on a conscious or subconscious level, to avoid any kind of exposure that would bring him face-to-face with shame or embarrassment. He is averse to vulnerability, to revealing his true self to another.

Because he is adept at connecting with others while keeping himself hidden, it appears that everyone knows him. He adapts to people and environments so well that others feel accepted by him and become accepting of him. But, the constant weight of protecting his hidden self from others can become so heavy that it can separate him from himself and from others.

Michael, who was deeply addicted to pornography, was a Chameleon. When he first came to see me, he stated that he wanted to work on his marriage to Amanda and his relationship with their children. I told him I would do my best to help him. For several weeks, Michael came to my office and talked about his wife and his children. He expressed bewilderment, frustration, and even anger about how hard life seemed. He never mentioned his addiction.

One day, Michael seemed unusually anxious when he came in for his counseling session. He stammered and stuttered through each sentence. Eventually, I leaned toward Michael and said, "I have the sense that you are trying to tell me something beyond what we are talking about. I have the feeling that you are talking about everything but what you want to talk about." Michael looked at me like a deer caught in headlights. I had never seen him so scared. He appeared to feel trapped.

Michael reluctantly said, "I need to tell you something I have never told anyone. I am addicted to pornography and have been for years. It is not just looking at pictures, but I have also engaged in phone sex and other kinds of pornographic Internet interactions with women. It has consumed my life. I have tried to stop, but cannot. I engage in some kind of Internet pornography every day." Michael shared his news like he was telling me about the latest weather pattern. He was emotionless except for a touch of relief he seemed to express when he was finished.

I responded, "Michael, I hear you, and I am glad you have chosen to be honest with me today. I am curious as to why you chose today to tell me ... why you decided to tell me at all?" Looking puzzled, he replied, "The more we have talked the last several weeks, the more I have become conscious of the secret of pornography I have kept hidden. As I have felt safer with you, I have shared more about my wife and things about our family; but I have, at the same time, become increasingly aware of protecting the secret of my addiction. You have helped me to feel safe and to know that I cannot expect to have a good relationship with Amanda without being honest. I want to get better."

Michael had taken an incredible risk. He had shown his true colors, not knowing what my response might be. On that day, Michael had made new friends of honesty and vulnerability. He had cast aside guilt and shame, the deceptive companions that had traveled with him for years and held him in bondage. He was now trying to break free.

New friends for a Chameleon = honesty and vulnerability

For a Chameleon such as Michael to risk being exposed is like what I imagine a real chameleon must feel when discovered on a white wall. In Mississippi, the chameleon will turn a bright green, becoming obvious to any onlooker. Knowing that, I can imagine that the chameleon feels some kind of panic wanting to run or find cover. The exposed chameleon must know he is no longer fooling anyone. The experience is one of death to the chameleon.

I looked directly at Michael and said as clearly as I knew how, "Michael, I am proud of your courage and your desire to become free. Acknowledging secrets is the beginning of many new possibilities for you. I want you to know that the greatest thing I see in you at this moment is NOT the fact that you are addicted to pornography. What I see is a man who wants to be free. I hope this is the beginning of a journey for you to become the Real You. I will do all I can to help you walk this path of healing."

King David was a Chameleon. David was the only man in all of Scripture to be described as "a man after God's own heart." And yet, when David fell into sin, he hid what he had done, lied to protect himself, and added layer upon layer of wrongdoing to cover one immoral act after another.

You remember the story from 2 Samuel 11 and 12 … One day during the spring, David stays in Jerusalem and doesn't go out to battle. While walking on the roof of his palace, he sees a beautiful woman. He sees Bathsheba, who was the wife of Uriah. He sends for her... has sex with her... and she becomes pregnant. David sends for Uriah who is on the battlefield and encourages him to go home to his wife, expecting that he will have sex with her. Uriah is so loyal to his men that he refuses and instead sleeps on the steps of the palace in honor of his men still on the battlefield. David, now desperate, has Uriah placed on the front-lines of the battle where he is killed. Nathan, God's spokesman, confronts David by telling him the story of a rich man who steals a lamb from a poor man and serves the lamb to a dinner guest. Listen to David's response to Nathan:

> Then David's anger burned greatly against the man,
> And he said to Nathan,
> "As the Lord lives,
> Surely the man who has done this deserves to die.
> And he must make restitution for the lamb fourfold,
> Because he did this thing and had no compassion."
> Nathan then said to David,
> "You are the man!"
> 2 Samuel 12:5-7

David knew what he had done, but he tried to hide the thing he needed to acknowledge. David chose the way of the Chameleon.

The Chameleon lives his life by hiding the things he knows about himself that he fears will be unacceptable to others.

WHAT DOES A CHAMELEON WANT?

A Chameleon wants to be accepted, to be liked, to fit in, and to be understood. He wants to blend into his environment with the least amount of strife or conflict. He works very hard to keep the peace, to help others get what they want. In so doing, he appears to be open, caring, and attuned to others in a good way. However, a Chameleon is not operating from his Real Self. In fact, his ability to identify with others can represent a desire to remain hidden rather than a willingness to be vulnerable and known by another.

Why does that work? It works because he manages to keep the focus on others and not on himself. He often skillfully connects with others by asking questions that express his interest and conveys his

> Chameleon = stay hidden or become vulnerable and known

deep regard for them. In most cases these are all great qualities. For the Chameleon, however, they are tools of self-protection that ultimately lead to isolation. Questions become a way of protecting the Chameleon from sharing himself. In this sense, the Chameleon has been referred to in our Men's Coaching Weekends as the Interviewer.

As the Interviewer, the Chameleon proves his interest by making sure his companion is busy talking about himself. Such interest is admirable in so many ways; however, the object of such close attention will ultimately feel the imbalance of the relationship. He will know that he has laid his self-disclosure cards on the table while the Interviewer has held his cards close to his chest and played none. While hiding behind an intense interest in another, the Interviewer makes no attempt to share himself. Real relationship is mutual sharing. The Interviewer wants to know you, but is unwilling to let you know him; he is unwilling to show his real colors.

My good friend Denny (Denny lost his battle with cancer while I was writing this. I miss my good friend.) and I eventually came to share openly, though he knew me as a Chameleon when we first met years ago. Denny was an outstanding dentist in the suburbs of Philadelphia. He grew up Jewish on the streets of this northeastern city. I grew up in the mountains and countryside of East Tennessee. Our backgrounds could not be more different.

We were the best of friends and shared our lives openly and honestly with one another. But, this is how Denny described many of the times we sat together when we first met. He said that I asked him many questions about himself, showing interest in the unique and different way he grew up on the streets of a large city. He felt like I was hiding my true self and that he often felt awkward when he left our time together. He had shared so much and I had shared so little of myself.

In some ways, I was aware of this and yet I perceived that my behavior meant I really cared about my friend. In that sense, I was genuinely seeking to build a deeper friendship. My motive was good, my relational skills were commendable, and the time we spent together flew by. These qualities were desirable and admirable, but I wasn't offering myself, open and vulnerable, to the relationship. Denny did not really know me. I knew lots about him, but the uneasiness in his gut when we ended our time together came from my lack of openness.

Ironically, this trait in me serves me well professionally. I show intense interest in my clients, ask questions that help them to be in touch with their lives, and listen intently as they fight through internal triggers that inhibit their own openness and healing. No one comes to see me professionally to hear me talk about me. I love helping others in this way, and I seem to satisfy most of the people who come to me for assistance.

The problem arises in my friendships and intimate relationships. When I choose to withhold my weaknesses or my struggles from peer-related conversations, I become detached and isolated in my own boat, adrift from the dock of closeness and connection with others who desire relationship with me. When I am not willing to risk telling close friends what I know is going on inside me, I create a wall that separates me from those who love and care about me. I find myself alone because I hide parts of myself that need healing and comfort. I choose to keep in secret what can only be healed when it is loved by another.

The wall = secrets that are not shared!

I share a little of my story to help you understand the nature of the Chameleon. The essence of the Chameleon is that he knows things about himself that he is unwilling to share for whatever reason. He is not as open and honest as he could be, which isolates him from a place of healing and freedom that would benefit him. Because he resists the honest and vulnerable communication that would foster intimate relationships, he opens himself to secrets, isolation, and destructive behavior.

The Chameleon wants relationship. As others get to know him, he begins to believe that if they knew him like he knows himself, they would think less of him. The Chameleon will find what he wants — acceptance and respect — when he chooses to pursue freedom through

> Chameleon = will find acceptance and respect through vulnerability in safe relationships!

vulnerable, open self-disclosure in safe, healing relationship.

King David acted as a Chameleon, and yet, when he was confronted by Nathan, he responded with great courage. Listen ...

> Then David said to Nathan,
> "I have sinned against the Lord."
> 2 Samuel 12:13

David was willing to take responsibility for the secrets. He acknowledged and owned his lies, his hiding, and his murderous ways.

A Chameleon will find the acceptance he longs for when he discovers safe relationship that will encourage him to share his life openly and vulnerably.

WHAT DOES A CHAMELEON FEAR?

The Chameleon is afraid that if the secrets he keeps about himself become known to others, they will find him unacceptable and reject him. He fears that he will lose what he has. He believes he cannot risk being known on an intimate level. He feels most secure in his self-protective mode, when in fact it prevents him from experiencing the healing power of being truly known by others. Not confronted, the fear of being fully known will drive him to dark places within himself.

> Secrets = destructive self-protection!

A gentleman named Wade came to the Men's Coaching Weekend hoping to gain something that would help put his life on a better path. Like so many men who come to our coaching weekend, Wade was already a successful entrepreneur who was beginning to branch out in new ways that promised to be profitable and satisfying. He was athletic, still in great shape even in his late 40s, and content with many opportunities he had to play all over the world in various kinds of recreational adventures.

The area in which Wade felt helpless was in his intimate relationships. He was recently divorced and had two teenagers, a son and a daughter. He did not know how to connect with his teenagers. He was lonely and lost, despite his ever-growing monetary success and his well-maintained physical condition. Wade did not know how to make his personal life match the success he enjoyed in other areas of his life.

By coming to the coaching weekend, Wade had placed himself in an environment that would be more than the typical teaching seminar. He heard men tell their stories of addiction or other harmful activities. Some who were not involved in destructive behaviors simply didn't know how to connect to their wives and children. They were lost and didn't know what to do.

As Wade listened intently to the stories openly shared by others, he found that their struggles and failures resonated with his own story. When he was invited to share his story, Wade began to describe himself to the other men. At first, he shared the basic information, such as where he lived, his professional accomplishments, his athletic success, and his worldwide traveling adventures. Then something seemed to change in Wade. He began sharing the pain of his divorce. He admitted that he never knew how to connect with his wife and that he never understood what she expected of him. "I would often come home and greet my wife, only to hear her ask me at some point in our conversation to tell her what was going on inside of me. When that happened, I immediately felt numb. I did not know what to do with that question. I did not know how to express my dissatisfaction with her, my life, and our marriage."

Wade went on to describe similar experiences with his teenagers. He never felt confident that he could really allow them to know what was going on inside of him. He never shared his fears, worries, or even his desires with his son. He never shared his dreams for his daughter. He shared neither his thoughts about them nor the bad stuff of his doubts and struggles. To his teenagers, Wade was distant, uninterested, and self-absorbed.

By the time Wade finished telling his story at the coaching weekend, he had shared a level of honesty about himself that he had never risked anywhere. He opened up to the other men in a way that exposed his doubts, his fears, and his weaknesses. He experienced genuine acceptance from the other men, not the rejection that he feared. No one made fun of him or shunned him for what he shared, but the fear of that happening had been very real to him.

He was surprised, even healed, by what he experienced. The men welcomed into a community of healing a part of Wade that he had hidden for years. Wade was moved to a place he had never been, a place of acceptance, vulnerability, and openness. No hiking trail, no whitewater raft trip, or mountain climbing adventure had ever given Wade this experience. When he courageously faced his fear of vulnerability, he found himself in a place of growth and healing.

Be open and vulnerable = find growth and healing!

Wade had never feared professional challenges, athletic tests, or the risk of any adventure. But, he feared the process of honestly facing and sharing what he knew was going on inside of him. He had even had panic attacks in past relationships when he sensed that he might be asked to do so.

The Chameleon fears the loss of his image, his assigned role to others, or his "bad stuff" being unacceptable to others. In the same way that the actual chameleon is a beautiful reptile, the personality of a Chameleon is often beautiful in the sight of others. But, his perception of himself does not allow him to expose himself easily. The Chameleon fears the sharing of Self will evoke some kind of dismissal by the people in his life. He gains acceptance and safety through his ability to blend in with others, but in so doing, he loses his distinctiveness, his Self.

Hide it, lose it! or Share it, find it!

You cannot expect to know your Self if you keep it hidden. To find your Life, you must open yourself to relationship. Jesus spoke to this paradox:

> For whoever wishes to save his life shall lose it,
> But whoever loses his life for My sake,
> He is the one who will save it.
> Luke 9:24

The man who overcomes his fear is a man who will find his Real Self. The Chameleon who conquers his fear of being exposed will be a free man. King David wrote the following:

> The Lord is my light and my salvation;
> Whom shall I fear?
> The Lord is the defense of my life;
> Whom shall I dread?
> When evildoers came upon me to devour my flesh,
> My adversaries and my enemies,
> They stumbled and fell.
> Though a host encamp against me,
> My heart will not fear;
> Though war arise against me,
> In spite of this I shall be confident.
> Psalm 27:1-3

The Chameleon lives in the fear of being exposed. Life is found through the exposure of Self to open, safe relationship. The Chameleon is afraid of that reality.

WHAT IS IT LIKE TO BE WITH A CHAMELEON?

A Chameleon can be a great friend and companion. His ability to join in and adapt to new people and circumstances is most appealing. Your wish is his desire. Having a companion who expresses great interest in you, asks questions about you, and invites you to talk about YOU is very satisfying. The Chameleon wants to know you, sincerely desires that you show your colors, and works deliberately to help you reveal yourself.

Being with a Chameleon = you share, he doesn't!

The problem arises when the Chameleon does not reciprocate the openness and vulnerability that he has invited you into. This may create discomfort in the relationship unless you are so narcissistic that being the focal point is all too gratifying and desirable. If you're a normal companion of the Chameleon, you begin to feel overexposed. The lack of openness from the Chameleon may move you to feelings of being alone, isolated, or abandoned. The sense of mutual openness is lost, and the Chameleon's style of hiding through joining himself to your color is exposed.

A guy named Stanley came to the Coaching Weekend after months of therapy. I invited Stanley to attend the Weekend hoping that he would learn how to connect to other men and share himself. He was reluctant but agreed to come. When Stanley arrived, he immediately began to relate to the stories of the men. He had no problem fitting in the group. He quickly seemed to be one of the most popular guys in the Weekend. All the other men seemed to genuinely like Stanley and welcomed him into any conversation that he entered. At one point in the Weekend, if we had stopped and voted on Most Popular, Stanley would have won hands down.

Stanley was enjoying the experience until he was invited to share his story with the other men. He seemed to lose the animation and openness that had so endeared him to the men. He stammered through the story of how his father had died when he was young and how his life had changed dramatically at that point. He reported it like the sun coming up in the east every morning. It was so matter-of-fact and so minimized in its affect that the other men were left puzzled as to how Stanley could report such pain but express so little emotion.

Stanley had come to see me privately because he was experiencing depression, lack of motivation, and little interest in his family or career. He felt lost. Even though he was a professional and at the height of his career, he had never felt so unfulfilled. In my office, Stanley had learned to share the story of the loss of his father and how his young life had been so altered by that event. He had even expressed some emotion at times, which led to a few tears of sadness and grief. Through the process, he had begun to experience some relief from his depression and a greater sense of direction in his life. And yet, he still was experiencing many of the symptoms that he longed to put behind him.

Stanley's wife, Julie, had found him to be more present and not so "lost in space," the way she had often experienced him. Julie had been drawn to Stanley because he was so caring and seemed so attuned to her every need. When they married, she watched Stanley give himself to the people in their church and community. Everyone loved Stanley, but Julie increasingly experienced Stanley as distant and often asked him to open up to her. He really didn't know what that meant. He could not understand that Julie wanted him to share his personal desires along with his feelings of pain and fear. She wanted to understand the values that revealed who Sam really was: His True Self.

In the Coaching Weekend, Stanley saw in the eyes of the men the same look that Julie had often given him: the look that says, "Where is Stanley? I hear what you are reporting, but I do not feel connected to you." The men asked Stanley if he was open to some feedback. Stanley reluctantly allowed the men to share what they experienced as they sat listening to his story. The men offered him something different than Julie or anyone else had ever given him. In this safe, accepting place, he received feedback about how the men saw him. While remaining truthful and direct, the men communicated to Stanley their understanding and approval. Here's a sample of what the men shared with Stanley as they gave him their honest assessment of what it was like to be in his presence:

- "I hear your report, Stanley, but I keep waiting on YOU to show up!"
- "I feel the pain of the loss of your father, but I wonder where that pain is in YOU!"
- "I keep wondering what you are hiding that is going on inside of you. I believe you are telling me the facts, but I do not believe you are connected to the story. You seem detached."
- "I see you, I hear you, but I do not feel connected to you. You seem flat in sharing what I believe to be a SAD story."

Notice how the men used "I" statements to reflect their experience of Stanley. They were not saying "you" are this way or that way. They honestly and without judgment, described how they experienced Stanley. Their feedback given in the context of acceptance and mutual openness, seemed to awaken Stanley from a deep sleep. His pain was exposed and contained within the lives of a group of men who cared for him and were not offering advice, only support and feedback. No man will be open unless he has a place he can talk freely and express his failures and fears. The support and care given to a man's weakness is the measure of true maturity, wholeness, and holiness. A grown-up man is a man who has experienced the acceptance of his brokenness, not just his gifts.

To be with a Chameleon can be fulfilling if you can invite him to share his life with you. He begins to find HIS color and not just the color of the people around him. The Chameleon finds he too has much color to offer in relationships. He knows how to adapt so well that he will lose himself in YOUR color.

To use an extreme example, being with a Chameleon can be like arriving at a nudist colony and finding that you are the only one not wearing clothes. You have bared yourself, but no one has reciprocated. You are likely to receive validation from a Chameleon, but you won't know the one who provided it.

A Chameleon can become a great friend once there is equal self-disclosure and openness in your relationship with him. Listen to the words of a recovering Chameleon:

> I'm feeling terrible—I couldn't feel worse!
> Get me on my feet again. You promised, remember?
> When I told my story, you responded;
> Train me well in your deep wisdom.
> Help me understand these things inside and out
> So I can ponder your miracle-wonders.
> My sad life's dilapidated, a falling-down barn;
> Build me up again by your Word.
> Barricade the road that goes Nowhere;
> Grace me with your clear revelation.
> I choose the true road to Somewhere,
> I post your road signs at every curve and corner.
> I grasp and cling to whatever you tell me;
> God, don't let me down!
> I'll run the course you lay out for me
> If you'll just show me how.
> Psalm 119:25-32 (The Message)

The Chameleon will be a better friend when he offers his true color to the relationship. He needs to let you see who he is. You will enjoy being with someone who offers himself fully and openly to the relationship.

WHAT DOES A CHAMELEON NEED TO DO TO CHANGE?

The Chameleon must learn to reveal himself to others. He needs to value and trust the sharing of himself openly and vulnerably. As the Chameleon learns to display the brilliant color of Self, rather than to reflect the color of others, he will emerge into the Special One he was designed to be. He must risk letting others know what he thinks, what he feels, what he values, what he desires, and what action he plans to take to fulfill his dreams. The Chameleon will change when he lets others know his True Color—his Real Self.

Chameleon = a huge risk: show his color!

In order for him to do that, he must find a safe, accepting person or group. Once in a group, he must recognize that his tendency to focus on others is a defensive behavior that prevents him from connecting with others. He must learn that all healthy and satisfying relationships require the revelation of his Real Self in order to thrive.

Moving away from the Chameleon as metaphor and looking at the chameleon as a reptile and animal reveals a helpful perspective on being real. Chameleons actually change colors as a response to the colors of their surroundings. Their ability to change colors is not about camouflaging themselves. Rather, their color changes in response to mood, temperature, and light. Their coloring is primarily a form of communication, such as whether or not they are willing to mate. So, in reality, seeing chameleons change colors is about revealing their true feelings. There is nothing deceptive about a chameleon changing colors.

Therefore, the Chameleon as metaphor understands that adapting and interacting with others is necessary for life. He must communicate. He must reveal. However, he does not realize that outwardly focusing on others while hiding his true self is destructive for him and for those in his life. He must be open to receiving the feedback from others and then begin to change by openly and honestly sharing with them. If the Chameleon can become vulnerable, then he can discover his Real Self.

The most difficult statements for a Chameleon may be words and phrases like:
- "I really am struggling with …"
- "I want so much to step into that direction, but I am afraid."
- "I have really messed up … this is what I've done."
- "I will share my life with you …"

Certainly, this kind of sharing is not easy for anyone. Not everyone necessarily likes to share on this intimate level. And yet, sharing on this level is necessary in order to become known and be Real.

In order to trust others with his true self, the Chameleon needs to feel he is in a safe place with accepting, non-judgmental people. He needs to know when he risks this level of openness that those around him will accept him and will not reject him. They must resist giving advice, expressing judgment, or displaying shock at his disclosure. No one grows in an environment of fear or condemnation and this is especially true for the Chameleon. He is very fearful that his disclosure will result in rejection or abandonment. His hope for change will flourish in an environment where he knows his self-revelations will not provoke negative responses.

The magic words "we are with you" become the scalpel in the relational surgery to free the heart of the Chameleon. He must find someone, a group, or friendships that can hear his self-disclosure and reflect love back to him.

King David models the courage to overcome the Chameleon in him.

Healing words = "We are with you!"

> I'm on the edge of losing it—
> the pain in my gut keeps burning.
> I'm ready to tell my story of failure,
> I'm no longer smug in my sin.
> My enemies are alive and in action,
> a lynch mob after my neck.
> I give out good and get back evil
> from God-haters who can't stand a God-lover.
> Psalm 38:16-18 (The Message)

The Chameleon who is ready for change will stop adapting to everyone around him and begin to risk offering his feelings, thoughts, and desires to the relationship. He will risk showing who he is.

> Finally, I confessed all my sins to you and stopped trying to
> hide my guilt.
> I said to myself, "I will confess my rebellion to the Lord."
> And you forgave me! All my guilt is gone.
> Psalm 32:4-6 (New Living Translation)

> Look at him;
> give him your warmest smile.
> Never hide your feelings from him.
> Psalm 34:5 (The Message)

> "Can anyone hide from me in a secret place?
> Am I not everywhere in all the heavens and earth?" says the Lord.
> Jeremiah 23:24 (New Living Translation)

> The Chameleon becomes a Lion when he begins the courageous revealing of himself.

CONCLUSION

The Chameleon knows others but others don't know him. He reflects the colors of the environment around him. His relating style is to identify more with his surroundings than to express himself assertively and openly. An important principle of life that especially applies to the Chameleon is this: "Anytime I am more attuned, more interested in, more aware of what another person thinks or values than I am aware of what I think or value, then I am out of balance."

I introduced you to Larry at the beginning of this chapter. Since I first met Larry he has grown in his ability to reveal himself and risk the exposure that made him a Chameleon. Larry is now able to take ownership for his behavior. He says things like:

- "I take responsibility for what I did."
- "I know I hurt you and this is how I understand what I have done to hurt you."
- "I want you to know what is going on inside me. I will reveal my deepest thoughts and fears to you."

Sign text: Chameleon = More attuned to others > awareness of Self

- "What I did was wrong, and this is what I am willing do to repair our relationship."
- "I have broken your trust in me. This is what I understand about how my behavior has hurt you."
- "I don't know how I have hurt you, but I want to know. I will listen. Please help me know what I have done to you."
- "I accept the pain I have brought to our relationship. I am committed to taking full responsibility for what I have done. I am not afraid of your anger or your sadness. I will not protect myself by hiding. Please help me know how I have hurt you."

Larry and Ellen have restored their relationship and are now experiencing more satisfaction than they had years ago. He is a different man because he is willing to reveal what is going on inside of him, instead of protecting himself and trying to control Ellen's disappointment or rejection. Larry offers his vulnerability to the relationship.

A person can only be genuinely giving when he is aware of his own need and then gives preference to another from that humble position. The Chameleon is often giving as a way to cope with the world, find identity and acceptance, and as a defense. This leaves the Chameleon in a dangerous place—too attuned to others and too identified with values that are not his own.

The Chameleon must learn to reveal what he likes or dislikes, and to risk the opposition from those who do not share his values. He must make a stand for his belief. He will only become Real when he risks the revelation of what he knows about himself and finds acceptance by others in that exposure.

Sign text: To eperience intimacy = you must be aware of your need!

A Chameleon changing colors is a beautiful sight. A Chameleon displaying his true color is a miracle. A Chameleon becoming a Lion is a courageous transformation!

REMEMBER THIS:

- The Chameleon hides.
- The Chameleon has hidden parts of himself that HE is aware of but is afraid to share these hidden parts with others.
- The Chameleon places himself in a dangerous place by holding onto the awareness of what he knows about himself that he fears sharing with another. The weight can become so heavy that it begins to separate him from himself and from others.
- The Chameleon wants to be accepted, liked, to fit in, and to be understood.
- The Chameleon will protect himself by keeping the focus on others.
- The Chameleon makes no attempt to share himself with the other person but hides behind an intense interest in the other person.
- The Chameleon fears vulnerable, honest communication to further his freedom and intimate relationship and thus opens himself to secrets, isolation, and destructive behavior.
- The Chameleon fears being exposed as something unacceptable. The Chameleon gains acceptance and safety through his ability to blend in with others, but in so doing, he loses his distinctiveness, his Self.
- The Chameleon can offer a fulfilling experience as a companion if he accepts your invitation to share his life with you.
- The Chameleon must learn to reveal himself to others. He needs to value and trust the sharing of himself openly and vulnerably.
- The Chameleon will become the Lion as he openly and vulnerably shares his life.

CHAPTER THREE
THE TURTLE

"He who knows not, and knows not that he knows not, is a fool ... shun him.
He who knows not, and knows that he knows not, is willing ... teach him.
He who knows, and knows not that he knows, is asleep ... awaken him.
He who knows, and knows that he knows, is wise ... follow him."
Omar Khayam (13th Century Philosopher)

Jesus said, "The one to whom I give this crust of bread after I've dipped it."
Then he dipped the crust and gave it to Judas, son of Simon the Iscariot.
As soon as the bread was in his hand, Satan entered him.
"What you must do," said Jesus,
"Do it and get it over with."
John 13:26-27

INTRODUCTION

The Turtle is the man who is unaware and unconscious of himself and others. He does not know his Self and is not known by Others. He is not relational and therefore not connected to a community, i.e. his family, friends, or profession. He may be functional in terms of task, but is inept when it comes to intimacy and closeness. He plays it safe and takes little risk and is not involved in adventure or exploring anything outside his comfort zone. He is unknown. Let me introduce you to a Turtle ...

Richard had no idea how he came across to others, what he offered to the group, or even why he was present at the Men's Coaching Weekend. He was oblivious to his place in the group. He simply showed up because I promised him that he would benefit.

The story of Richard is the story of the Turtle. Richard was present in body, but seemed to be out of step with all parts of his life. He did not talk much, he offered little to his family or friends, and he seemed to hold back at work. He did not know how to engage socially, and he did not know how to reach out to others. The energy around him seemed to be more like a vacuum. Any power was absorbed in his unaware and unconscious existence.

There seemed to be a shell that protected him and prohibited him from experiencing life. He could not be touched or reached. His movements, emotionally and physically, seemed slow and weighty. His presence felt heavy and strained, rather than lighthearted and inviting.

Oddly enough, Richard seemed to come alive when the topic of conversation was on the untouchable topics of politics or religion. Anything personal left him clueless. He had no self-awareness, no ability to form a sentence about his personal life. He was clearly more comfortable speaking from his head than speaking from his heart. It was not that he consciously avoided speaking from his heart; he just did not know how to do so. He had no friends, and yet it wasn't as if anyone hated him or was his enemy.

Richard had often heard his wife make statements like, "There is no life in this relationship. I am bored. You work all the time. You provide for us, but it's like you are not present. Where are you?" Richard did not know how to respond to such statements. He was unaware of how his life affected his wife and others around him. He was responsible in tasks, but unable to connect relationally to his wife and friends.

For Richard, life was in neutral, and he was driving a car headed steadily downhill. He was being carried along, working hard to stay out of the ditch, but with no direction, no intent, and no purpose. Even though he read a lot, he was not growing. And, though there was no conflict, he was not moving closer to his wife and children. His wife was lonely and dissatisfied in their marriage, but he was not unhappy. In the absence of any obvious problem, he could not understand why others were so frustrated by him.

HOW IS A MAN LIKE A TURTLE?

A man is like a Turtle when he is unaware of key characteristics, traits, and behaviors that have negative consequences for his relationships with family, friends, and associates. Unlike the other types, where at least one side of the relationship is aware, no one knows the heart of the Turtle. He does not know himself, and therefore, others cannot know him. He plays it safe and is unwilling to take risks. The Turtle does not trust.

Turtle = unaware and unconscious of self and others

The Turtle is the man who is so focused on function that he is blind to how others experience him or even how he experiences himself. He is often steady, stable, non-reactive, and predictable. The Turtle offers a framework for life that is characterized by no surprises. In fact, life is so safe with a Turtle that if the safety gets any greater, falling asleep is a real possibility for those trying to relate to him. To say life with a Turtle can be boring is stating the obvious.

For him, however, his personal need for security and safety is more valuable than a full and exciting life. The Turtle, as is shown by the Diagram, is blind to who he is and how others experience him. His life is lived in the unconscious. He seems to sleepwalk through life as it relates to self and others. He may be exceptional in some sort of ability or skill, but even then, he

Turtle = safe but boring

SELF

	KNOWN	NOT KNOWN
OTHERS KNOWN	Lion	Bull
OTHERS NOT KNOWN	Chameleon	Turtle • UNAWARE • UNCONSCIOUS OF SELF AND OTHERS • NO RISK • NO ADVENTURE

DIAGRAM FOUR

will be unaware of his gifts. The UNKNOWN swallows his Self and his relationships like a black hole.

Jake was the classic Turtle. He came to the Men's Coaching Weekend unaware of what he wanted to find. Life was not working, but he couldn't figure out why. The feedback he received from his wife, his teenage son, and his friends told him he was out of touch with them. He could not figure out what they wanted from him. Were they mad at him? Were they unreasonable in their critique of him? Were they truly aligned against him? Jake was lost!

Surprisingly, he was willing to risk coming to be with other men in a weekend retreat. He was so confused. At first, Jake began to experience the men as he did his family. He was uncomfortable, felt out of place, and wanted to leave. He couldn't determine if they were mad at him or trying to get him to do something he would never be able to do.

Jake could tell you his name, what he did for a living, and the names of his children. That happened to be the extent of his ability for personal sharing. When the conversation was directed to Jake's profession as a computer analyst, he could respond. He could passionately address the outlook for the college football team of his Alma mater. But, he had no ability to share personally. He could not recognize his strengths, nor could he admit his weaknesses. The problem for Jake was the fact that he did not see a problem with that. After all, he wasn't missing something that he was looking for.

Because a person can't feel the absence of an ability they can't comprehend, he didn't know he wasn't connected in a meaningful way with his family or with the men at the retreat. How could there be a problem when there was really no problem? For the Turtle, there is no awareness of the loss of being known by others. He does not consciously long for a better understanding of himself. Feedback from others is like a foreign language to him. He hears noise, can even make out some of the words, but he is unsure of what is really being communicated. He feels no need for more contact or for a greater reality of being known.

Turtle = no awareness of what's missing!

The Turtle is simply living in the unconscious.

He has blind spots that prevent him from seeing the good things about himself as well as the bad things about himself. The Turtle is unaware of his abilities, his aptitude, or skills. He is unaware of what he fears or what his aversions are. He is most likely withdrawn in his feelings. He has learned a way to survive, and it has worked for him. His shell is comfortable and he knows it well. He only trusts in what he can see, what he can touch, what he can control.

AND THEREIN LIES THE PROBLEM!

Judas Iscariot, the man who betrayed Jesus, was a Turtle. Judas had no consciousness as to what he was doing in taking 30 pieces of silver to identify Jesus to the Pharisees and Roman soldiers. When he did realize what he had done, it was too late.

> Judas, the one who betrayed him,
> realized that Jesus was doomed.
> Overcome with remorse,
> he gave back the thirty silver coins to the high priests,
> saying, "I've sinned. I've betrayed an innocent man."
> They said, What do we care? That's your problem!"
> Judas threw the silver coins into the Temple and left.
> Then he went out and hung himself.
> Matthew 27:3-5

Judas failed. He did not know himself and others did not know him. Judas was in that place of, "I don't know and you don't know," unconscious and unaware. LOST!

WHAT DOES A TURTLE WANT?

Turtle = safety is greatest value!

The Turtle wants to feel safe. He wants emotional safety while feeling nothing. He has evolved into a hard-shelled man in order to protect himself from the chaos and hurt that he has long forgotten or chosen not to remember. The unconscious vow to be safe has alienated him from self and others. He has chosen safety over growth. Turtles get older, fatter, and more predictable, but they do not risk, do not explore, and do not seek new adventures. The Turtle values safety above all else.

I live in Mississippi where our plentiful lakes and small ponds abound with turtles. My regular exercise routine of race-walking takes me around the lake behind my home where I will often see 15 or more turtles lined up on a single log sticking out of the water. As soon as one turtle catches a sense of my presence, all the turtles dive off the log into the water. They all swim for safety ... no curiosity, no exploring, and no risk. I often imagine the first one that hears something to say to the other turtles, "Go! Get out of here ... something is coming!" None of the other turtles question the first turtle. At the first sign of danger, they flee. A turtle values safety above all else.

The man who is a Turtle wants life to work, but without vulnerability and openness. He values safety so much that he removes any sense of adventure from his life. He chooses the self-protection of his shell to shield himself from risk and potential harm. In so doing, he loses touch with important life elements such as exploration, curiosity, and a desire to understand the world around him. He pulls into his shell and becomes disconnected from the people and culture surrounding him.

Turtle = no adventure!

"I want to be safe! I want to be safe! I want to be safe!" The Turtle chants that mantra unconsciously over and over in his head. He is committed to feel no pain. He wants to have no disruptions to his life. He demands the organization of his life to be free of surprise. He values predictability and certainty. He clings to the log of the known and will dive into the water of safety at the first sign of danger from the unknown.

Jimmy was a Turtle who sat motionless at the orientation to the Men's Coaching Weekend. He looked like he might vomit at any moment. At one point, I really thought he might bolt from his chair and make a run for it. Not that anyone would have prevented him from leaving at any time; it was just clear that his discomfort was at a high level. Jimmy had never placed himself in such an environment.

When one of the other men asked him why he had come to the Coaching Weekend, he replied, "I trusted Phil, and my wife thought

I would benefit. I did not want to come, but my marriage is in such a difficult place. I knew I needed to do something!" Jimmy would never have placed himself in such a vulnerable position unless there was pain in his life. The reality of his wife's dissatisfaction and of his not knowing what to do had led him to do something different. He was scared and anxious.

As Jimmy crawled through the weekend, he slowly began to open up to the group. He admitted that his personal mantra was, "the path of least resistance." He said that whenever he experienced tension, conflict, or challenge with his wife, he always chose the path of least resistance. He would disengage, head in a different direction, and find his safety in solitude. He would not confront, dialogue, or explore how a circumstance with his wife could be better. The more his wife complained, the more he ran for cover.

For Jimmy to see this truth about himself was remarkable. How can someone know what he does not know? How does a Turtle come to understand that his style is robbing him of life when he is experiencing no discomfort, no want for more, and has no incentive to change anything? HE MUST ENGAGE! The Turtle has built such a shell around his heart that he knows no other way and has no longing for something different. Jimmy was beginning to become conscious of how unknown he was to himself and to those around him. He was seeing and hearing things about himself that he had previously been blind to. Jimmy the Turtle was learning to be real, to be the Lion by staying engaged with the other men.

WHAT DOES A TURTLE FEAR?

As I walk around my neighborhood lake that provides an idyllic setting for exercise walking, I often ask myself this question. "What does a Turtle fear?" Turtles fear inadequacy. They fear that the part of them that is protected behind their shell will be exposed and will somehow be inadequate to handle whatever or whoever it is that faces them.

Turtle = fears inadequacy!

The Turtle is unaware of how he has traded adventure, exploration, and risk for safety. He has found a place of comfort and he is not missing the part of his life that has been lost. He has ultimately traded the ability to move into the world assertively and creatively as an image bearer of God for the pursuit of personal safety and comfort. The message inside his head is intended to be "CHARGE!" However, inside his head he hears, "PLAY IT SAFE!" and that is the message that wins out.

The Turtle is rarely able to face his fears unless he is confronted by such discomfort that he is forced to begin dealing with his life in a different way. As long as avoidance and hiding are working, there is no need for the Turtle to change. The Turtle will not find even counseling to be helpful until he values the feedback from those around him so much that he is willing to explore the message that he is getting from others.

At some point, he must make a quantitative shift. He must place a higher degree of value on what others are saying to him than on what he believes to be true. As long as he is anchored to the safety and comfort that protects and prevents him from seeing the big picture, he will remain unknown and unaware of what is missing in his life and why others feel so little connection to him.

Turtle = must stop avoidance and hiding!

Jason was the typical Turtle. He came to the Men's Coaching Weekend reluctantly. His wife was frustrated with how Jason was handling his life. The man that she married seemed to have disappeared. Jason was different now. She reported that Jason was depressed and withdrawn. She was tired of feeling like she was caring for another child. She wanted the man she fell in love with to come home. Jason was bewildered by what Karen was telling him.

At the Coaching Weekend, Jason was now with a group of men who were strangers to him. Initially, all the men seemed so much more aware of themselves and what they needed to do to make life work for them. But, as the men began to share the stories of their lives, Jason's attitude changed. He heard the men sharing openly and honestly how life was hard, how they had failed, and how they were facing their fears. Jason found himself both drawn to the openness but also scared to death. He was being exposed to a new way of life by listening and watching other men put words to the good, bad, and ugly parts of their lives.

It was time to share so Jason began sharing HIS story. He shared how he felt unfulfilled in his profession, how his wife seemed disappointed with him, and how he felt no passion about any part of his life. He could not remember the last time he was excited about something. He shared openly how he had worked so hard to be a nice guy and how life worked so well for him until recently. NICE wasn't working for him any longer.

As Jason began sharing more about his past, he shared about his father. "My Dad died from cancer when I was 12. I didn't know what to do or where to turn. I felt lost. My Mom seemed to need me more. I began giving my attention to her needs. I chose to do what she wanted me to do. I didn't want to cause problems for her because she was confronted with so much when my Dad died. My Mom depends on me a lot." Jason shared this story of his childhood with less emotion than someone reporting on paint drying.

The other men listened to his story. It was obvious that all the men felt more of Jason's pain and sadness than Jason did. When Jason finished his story, the men began offering feedback. Man after man reflected sadness for a little boy who lost his Dad at a critical time in his life. Another man shared how he felt anger toward Jason's mother for seeming to draw Jason into such a close relationship with her and appearing to ask Jason for more than he could give: "No 12-year-old boy who has just lost his father should be made to think he is responsible for the care of his mother." Jason was stunned by the level of emotion and care he was experiencing from the men.

The men were offering acceptance and truth in a way that Jason could receive it. He found an environment where he felt safe to explore areas of his life that were hidden and frozen. He heard men share openly and vulnerably about their lives. Jason found courage enough through the men's stories to share his own. When he shared his own story, that's when he truly began to benefit. He saw in the

> Turtle = must recognize: self-awareness comes from connection to others!

eyes of the men a level of emotion that he had never experienced about his own life. As he took in the experiences of the other men, he became aware of the parts of himself to which he had been blind. Seeing his life from the perspective of the other men was the first step in Jason's journey to self-awareness. He was becoming known to the men by sharing his story. He was becoming known to himself through the feedback of a group of men who only hours before had been strangers to him.

The Turtle is caught in a catch-22. He is afraid of being found inadequate. And yet, he will never grow if he does not risk becoming conscious of his faults or his gifts. If he continues to run from others, hide his own experience, and avoid all uncomfortable environments, he will remain immature and undeveloped in significant areas of his growth. The strategy that once protected him will be the very reason that those around him will lose their sense of contact with him. A survival strategy serves a person well during a crisis, but it will hinder life if continued indefinitely. For growth to occur, fear must be faced. As with the other styles, the Turtle must also overcome the fear of being open and vulnerable. As he safely discovers his unknown self, he will become aware of the areas he needs to change to improve his enjoyment of his life and relationships.

> Turtle = fear of openness and vulnerability!

I recently experienced something different in my walk around the neighborhood lake. As I approached a large log, I saw more than 20 turtles lined up, shell to shell. When I got to the familiar place where they could hear me, all the turtles but ONE dove for the water. I stopped and waited for the last turtle on the log to follow all the others into the safety of the water. He never moved. I stood and admired his courage. He was different. I imagined him as the turtle all the other turtles respected. He was the brave turtle...the turtle who faced his fear!

WHAT IS IT LIKE TO BE WITH A TURTLE?

Boring! The Turtle plays it so safe that he risks little, lives in his head, and never exposes his struggles or vulnerability. He is most likely to have an intense interest in a non-relational topic, i.e. sports, music, career, or even theology. There is nothing wrong with those interests except when they are used as escapes or as some kind of false source for life. When an interest or ability has the power to protect a Turtle from his relationship with you, there is a major problem. The Turtle is more connected to SOMETHING than SOMEONE! He is NOT interested in being known by you or by others. His commitment is to comfort and safety. Trust outside himself is impossible.

Turtle = connection to something > connection to someone

Being with a Turtle leaves you longing for someone who cares about you. The Turtle is so disconnected from personal relationship that he does not feel the loss, but YOU do! Your experience is the feeling of being abandoned for the material, the non-relational. The Turtle's energy pursues an object or interest that involves his thinking, but not his feeling. The only feeling the Turtle is conscious of is whatever alerts him to danger. Therefore, to feel is to fear. The Turtle thinks to himself, "If it's about feeling, then run." Therefore, YOU feel the absence of a true friend or partner.

Turtle = little emotion, little connection!

Because the Turtle has learned to fear his emotions and deny their importance, he is unconscious of what you are experiencing in his presence. There is little emotion in the Turtle; therefore, you are left with no handle that holds you to him. It's like being on the subway and standing up with no handrail to hold onto. Your experience is stressful because there is no connection. You are alone in trying to bring balance to the instability of the relationship. A wise companion with a Turtle would say, "I need you to show up, to be in this relationship, to be present!" When you do, you are asking the Turtle to begin working with his

Turtle = expose his avoidant behavior!

emotions, which is confusing and frightening to him. Your request is appropriate. The problem is that you are asking the Turtle to do something he does not know how to do.

Being with a Turtle requires you to expose him to his avoidant behavior. You must confront him without criticism or blame. The challenge is to expose him to his defensive strategies in a way the keeps him from "diving off the log into the water." The Turtle will not grow until someone like YOU offers him safety outside his shell while exposing him to his self-defeating ways. You must provide the emotional safety to which he so desperately clings and for which he believes he alone is responsible. Can YOU do that? Are YOU that SOMEONE?

I am always amazed watching a Turtle experience for the first time the acceptance offered by others at the Men's Coaching Weekend. Each man becomes the person who reflects the safety that the Turtle has worked so hard to create for himself.

Matt was such a man. He came to the Weekend with guilt and shame from years of struggling with pornography. He and his wife had been in counseling for most of their 15-year marriage. Matt was offered the opportunity to tell the story of his life. With his head down and rubbing the palms of his hands back and forth, he shared with the men how he had become exposed to pornography when he was ten years old. Since that day he had fought his cravings for comfort with the short-lived pleasure of pornography. He had no concept of how his wife or children experienced him, no awareness of his own real desires. His primary feeling was for sex. He had become a Turtle: unaware and unconscious of his need to be known by another and to know someone else.

Matt shared how his view of sex from all the exposure to pornography had affected intimacy with his wife. He had thought that his struggle with pornography would be over when he got married. Sadly, he found that his sexual appetite was not satisfied with his wife. Even when she was willing to have sex six or seven times per week, he could not be satisfied. The urges seemed to only increase. This left him angry and frustrated. He criticized his wife and blamed her for his lack of satisfaction. He complained that she was wrong for not having the sexual appetite that he did.

I began wondering what Matt's wife must think of him ... or of herself ... or of the marriage: "What would it be like being married to Matt?" My respect for his wife grew progressively as I listened to Matt tell his story. I experienced my heart going out to Matt and, at the same time, I felt a significant admiration for his wife. Being Matt's wife would be a challenge!

Matt was sharing as openly and honestly as I have ever heard a man share. Interestingly, the setting from which Matt was sharing was a pontoon boat in the middle of a lake, where he sat telling his story to the group of men surrounding him on the boat. When Matt finished, the men began to offer feedback to him. They shared statements such as:

- "I admire your courage to be so open with us!"
- "I am sad for you, for the loneliness you have lived with."
- "I am amazed that your wife has not asked you to leave."
- "I hurt for you."
- "I hear your struggle."

The men's comments were honest, as they spoke from their guts. They held nothing back. Without being judgmental or shaming, I asked him what it was like for him to share so openly and experience safety and acceptance from the other men. Matt's response surprised me: "It's like working outside on a hot summer day, being very hot and sweaty, then coming into a cool place and having someone offer you a cool drink of water!" I sat quietly, as did the other men, and allowed Matt's words to soak into our beings. "I hear you, Matt ... I hear you," we were saying to him. We sat with Matt as he experienced the safety of "sitting on that log."

I then said, "Matt, look around you right now and tell me what you see." Matt looked up reluctantly and replied, "I see a group of men who seem to care about me, who are not condemning me." I said, "Matt, these men accept you for who you are. They want you to feel safe. They want you to find a better way than pornography or sex to feel like a man. They are offering you grace so that you can begin to grow into the man God designed you to be. I want you to look beyond them and tell me what you see." Matt took a survey of the men, then the boat, and then he scanned the water and the immense lake the boat was floating upon. "I see water all around me," he said. I looked Matt in the eyes and said, "Matt, I want you to remember this moment. There is more water surrounding you than you could drink in a lifetime. This water represents the grace that is offered to you if you will simply offer yourself openly and vulnerably. We love you and care about you!"

The next week, I received this email from Matt. "I continue to go to the time on the pontoon boat on the 'sea of grace' when struggling with negative thoughts…it takes a little effort, but it shuts down the negative like a charm." I would never say that Matt was cured from his addiction or healed in his struggles to experience intimacy with his wife. But, he began to accept the risk of being known and of learning to receive the acceptance he desperately needed to enjoy the life he longed for.

On some level, addiction is always about pain and loss that has never been faced and grieved. Matt had come out of hiding … he had crawled out of his shell … he had risked the possibility of being rejected to find the safety and acceptance he needed through a group of men on a pontoon boat.

Turtle = consumed by danger!

The Turtle is not an enjoyable person to be with because he is cut off from himself and others. He is very consumed by his experience of the danger and pain of life. He has not developed through open, vulnerable relationship what is necessary for real growth. Being with a Turtle is to experience his cold, hard outer shell while YOU long to know the soft inside that seems so lost or non-existent.

WHAT DOES A TURTLE NEED TO DO TO CHANGE?

For the Turtle, the most significant challenge to change is that he has no conscious need for change. He is content to "sun on his log" indefinitely. As long as his self-created safety works for him, he will not change. He has most likely constructed a reasonably workable life. His interests feed his need for stimulation, and his contact with the world is controlled. The Turtle has learned a way of relating that minimizes risk. Therefore, the Turtle will not change if SOMEONE does not call him out of his comfort zone. Jesus said it well here:

> That's what I mean:
> Risk your life and get more than you ever dreamed of.
> Play it safe and end up holding the bag.
> Luke 19:26 (The Message)

In order to change, the Turtle must become aware of the blind spots that prevent him from being connected to himself and others. In the absence of self-discovery, he has not experienced the types of validation that bring self-correction to his life. He has minimal, shared discovery experiences such as being a significant part of a team or group. The idea of being openly and intuitively observed by others is foreign at best and most likely terrifying and unwanted. The Turtle must venture into waters where he has no intrinsic motivation to go. SOMEONE must push him to discover the lost parts of himself. He was designed for more than a Turtle's life. He must begin to see the Turtle's way of relating is a maladaptive style that is robbing him of his life.

Turtle = too comfortable!

For example, Matt was designed for more than pornography or sex with his wife. And yet, his life had become consumed by his way of being a Turtle. His addiction fed his longings, and he resisted any kind of exposure of what he was really feeling or thinking. There was so much to Matt's story that he had never told anywhere, not even in my counseling office.

Turtle = robbed of life!

As Matt finished telling his story on the pontoon boat in the presence of the other men, I asked him if he had ever told these things to anyone else. Matt had shared for the first time how he longed for contact with his father, but his father was a stern, rigid man. He never experienced his dad as caring or helpful. His father rarely talked to him unless it was about giving him direction or barking out some kind of punishment. Matt did what any young boy does—he survived! He was unconscious of his longings for closeness and validation from his father.

Matt adapted to this loss in two typical ways. First, he swallowed the pain of lost relationship with his dad and filed the loss under the unconscious file of WHAT'S WRONG WITH ME? Somehow his pain seemed to tell a story that something was wrong with him. The message usually goes something like this: IF I WERE BETTER, MY DAD WOULD WANT TO SPEND TIME WITH ME. Second, Matt developed an anger problem. Anger will always surface at a time of loss. Anger is the emotion of loss. Anger offers to be your friend.

Unfortunately, anger as a friend under these circumstances usually metastasizes into some kind of emotional cancer because it has no healthy expression. The anger offers a form of power in a powerless circumstance. It could be a good thing, but it rarely is because it does not get spoken as an assertive expression of one's self. The anger becomes more about a protest to unmet needs than about the healthy expression of desire, and therefore, gets expressed as criticism and resentment.

Several weeks after Matt sat on the pontoon boat, I invited the Men's Group for dinner on my patio. My wife had designed an outdoor space with fireplace, grill area, ceiling fans, and water feature. It is a great open-air men's meeting space. As we finished dinner, one of the men invited Matt to read a letter that the group knew Matt had been struggling to complete for sometime. He was seeking to give an assertive expression to the voice of anger and pain that had so fueled his search for comfort through pornography and sex.

Matt agreed to read what he had written. He began reading and very quickly began to weep. Matt's letter was honest, vulnerable, and revealing. Here was a man who was giving a voice to pain and loss that happened years ago. No amount of pornography or sex with his wife was enough to soothe the hurt of a little boy who longed for his Dad. As Matt continued to read, his weeping turned to full crying. He had to stop to catch his breath. Matt was entering the room of healing through grief and sadness. The comfort he had sought through pornography was now becoming legitimate as he experienced the support and care from the men around the patio.

Matt finished reading his letter. He dried his eyes and apologized for the tears: "I am surprised that I was so emotional. I have never done that!" I asked, "Do you wish you hadn't cried?" "NO, I am not ashamed that I cried; it actually felt good even though it was hard. I am just surprised because I had no idea that I really felt that way." I reflected to Matt that he had never faced his hurt that way and that he had never given the hurt from his past such an opportunity of expression.

> Turtle = can find life through grief and sadness!

I asked Matt to work with me for a moment. I placed two cups in front of him. In one, I poured water. In the other, I poured wine. (I knew Matt did not drink any alcoholic beverage.) I asked Matt which he preferred. As I expected, he answered, "I prefer the water." I complimented Matt on his choice. Water is a good thing! I pulled the water cup away and then asked Matt what he would do if he were thirsty and the water cup was not available. "What would you drink, Matt?" Matt sat quietly for a few minutes trying to decide when all of us knew he didn't really have a choice. What do you do when you have no choice? Matt was in a double-bind.

He was thirsty, but he didn't like wine. After the long pause, Matt reluctantly spoke, "I would choose the wine." I sat quietly and allowed Matt's choice to sink in for him. "Matt, the water is like your dad. You were designed to have your thirst quenched by what your Dad would offer you in teaching and nurturing you into manhood. The wine is like the pornography and sex. You tried to quench your thirst through the false comfort of pornography and sex. That kind of wine will never satisfy when you were designed for water. Matt got it. The Turtle was courageously facing his pain.

The Turtle needs to become aware of what he has lost. He will not change until he begins to value the parts of himself that have been lost due to pain or lack of validation. The shell of self-protection has created safety, but, in so doing, has created a deadness that is manifested in unconscious and unaware behavior. Unless the Turtle is exposed to SOMEONE who helps him see, who creates safety for

Turtle = must become aware of what has been lost!

him, who calls him out of hiding, and who offers him real comfort, he will continue to live in an isolated condition.

The Turtle can change with help. He, especially, of the three quadrants (the Bull, the Chameleon, and the Turtle) is characterized by lack of knowledge. He needs SOMEONE. If you think you might be a Turtle, you must ask for help. If you are with a Turtle, you must expose the Turtle to his hidden parts. The Turtle will only change when he is willing to evaluate himself according to what he was designed to be, not what he experiences.

Turtle = live by design, not experience!

A Turtle can become a Lion by placing himself in a community of relationship that invites him to trust others, receive their help, and begin to reveal what he is learning about the world around him. All of that requires RISK for the Turtle. He must get off his log and begin to explore. He must enter into the adventure, the journey for which he was designed. He must learn to trust.

Listen to the words that invite the Turtle to move....

> I'm proud to praise God, proud to praise God.
> Fearless now, I trust in God;
> What can mere mortals do to me?
> Psalm 56:9-11 (The Message)

> My help and glory are in God
> —granite-strength and safe-harbor-God—
> So trust him absolutely, people;
> lay your lives on the line for him.
> God is a safe place to be.
> Psalm 62:6-8 (The Message)

The Turtle has resources that can help him move away from his self-protective, unconscious, and unaware strategy. Can a Turtle become a Lion? Yes! Transformation is possible, for God promised!

> Now we look inside,
> and what we see is that anyone united with the Messiah
> gets a fresh start, is created new.
> The old life is gone; a new life burgeons! Look at it!
> 2 Corinthians 5:17 (The Message)

CONCLUSION

"He who knows not, and knows not that he knows not, is a fool … shun him."

The opening line of the quote from Omar Khayam, a 13th century philosopher, describes the experience of the Turtle. He works to ensure that those around him stay away from areas in which he needs growth. He hides and protects so much of himself. Those around him often allow him to remain unaware and unexposed to areas that he knows not and knows not that he knows not. He is a fool if he continues to live in such an unknown place. He needs help!

The Turtle is truly in a dilemma. He is confronted by a reality of which he is unconscious and unaware. How can he change something that he feels no need to change? His strategy is so much about protection and survival that risk has no place in his life. The Turtle has no real sense of growth or need to grow.

The Turtle will NOT move to a better place until he allows himself to become involved and connected to another or others who offer safety, invite exposure, and provide support for extending his experience of the world. He must move off the log and begin to experience the fear within himself that typically holds him back. This never happens intrinsically; it requires someone or something outside of himself to push him into a place of growth. This push often occurs when the Turtle loses his log as a result of a change of circumstance or a confrontation from someone who can no longer live with his style. As long as the Turtle has his place of comfort, there will be no change. Take away his log, and he is forced to move into a different place.

The Turtle is enslaved by his blind spots. He must be open to others' observation and feedback in order to see those unknown things about himself and the world around him. He must venture into a path of self-discovery and learn the joy of growth. His motivation to change will occur only when an external source forces him to consider something new. The Turtle especially needs someone in his life that will invite him into a place of growth. What has been damaged in relationship can only be healed in relationship.

The Turtle needs someone to call him to a place of growth — a place of exploring, curiosity, and seeking to understand.

He needs YOU!

REMEMBER THIS:

- The Turtle takes no risk.
- The Turtle is unaware and unconscious of areas of his life that call for growth.
- The Turtle feels no need for more contact or for a greater reality of being known.
- The Turtle's unconscious commitment to be safe has left him alienated from self and others.
- The Turtle chooses safety over growth.
- The Turtle does not risk, does not explore, and does not seek new adventure.
- The Turtle must learn to engage and to trust!
- The Turtle fears inadequacy.
- The Turtle will not change as long as avoidance and hiding are working.
- The Turtle must place a higher value on what others are saying to him than what he believes to be true.
- The Turtle is more connected to SOMETHING than SOMEONE!
- The Turtle will change only if SOMEONE calls him out of his comfort zone.
- The Turtle will change only when he is willing to evaluate himself according to what he was designed to be, not what he experiences.
- The Turtle can be a Lion if he begins to risk and to trust.

CHAPTER FOUR
THE LION

> And this is the real and eternal life:
> That they know you, the one and only true God,
> And, Jesus Christ, whom you sent.
>
> John 17:3 (The Message)

"Real isn't how you are made," said the Skin Horse. "It's a thing that happens to you. When a child loves you for a long, long time, not just to play with, but REALLY loves you, then you become Real." "Does it hurt?" asked the Rabbit. "Sometimes," said the Skin Horse, for he was always truthful. "When you are Real you don't mind being hurt." "Does it happen all at once, like being wound up," he asked, "or bit by bit?" "It doesn't happen all at once," said the Skin Horse. "You become. It takes a long time. That's why it doesn't happen often to people who break easily, or have sharp edges, or who have to be carefully kept. Generally, by the time you are Real, most of your hair has been loved off, and your eyes drop out and you get loose in your joints and very shabby. But these things don't matter at all; because once you are Real you can't be ugly, except to people who don't understand."

Margery Williams from The Velveteen Rabbit

Mufasa: "You have forgotten who you are and so have forgotten me. Look inside yourself, Simba. You are more than what you have become. You must take your place in the Circle of Life."
Simba: "How can I go back? I'm not who I used to be."
Mufasa: "Remember who you are. You are my son and the one true king. Remember …"

From The Lion King

"If God fights in us, who can resist us?
There is a stronger lion in us than that against us."
Charles Spurgeon from Day by Day Devotional

INTRODUCTION

The Lion is all about knowing and being known. He knows himself, is aware of Self. He is known by others, is open to the Group. He seeks to know others and allow others to know him. He lives in community by offering himself and receiving from those around him. He is fully engaged in becoming all he was designed to be. He is courageously tackling all aspects of life.

Let me introduce you to a man who wants to be a Lion.…

Joe came into my office and sat down. He was visibly uncomfortable. I had spoken to a large group of which Joe and his wife were a part. Something I said had prompted Joe's wife, Sally, to nudge Joe into counseling. Sally was hoping that Joe would finally learn how to connect with her. Joe was confused. He was a good provider. He was a professional in his career, a good father, and well-respected in the community and in his church. To many of his friends, he was the model of what a man should be.

We exchanged greetings. Joe and I knew each other as friends and now he was getting ready to ask for my help professionally. I asked, "What would you like me to help you with, Joe?" "Sally wants me to learn how to share myself with her," he said. He could hardly form the words. He said them as if Sally had forced him to memorize them. He had no idea what the words meant. He was bewildered by her request and somewhere between offended and embarrassed that he was sitting in my office in such a humiliating position.

Joe was lost. He loved Sally enough to honor her nudge and be in my office; and yet, he would have been more comfortable in a Russian language class or a bull riding competition. I asked Joe to describe his life with Sally. He stumbled through a story that I have heard many times before and since.

"Sally says I don't share myself with her, and I am out of touch with what is really going on inside me. She wants me to be more open with her about my thoughts and feelings. I have no clue as to how she expects me to be a man and be in touch with myself so I can keep her in touch with me. I'm not in touch with ME; how can I keep HER updated? Sally wants to be closer to me, but I don't know how to make that happen."

Joe had no idea what being close to Sally really meant. He knew how to provide for the physical needs of Sally and his family. He and Sally even had a reasonably good sex life, but knowing how to really connect to Sally in a relational way was missing. Joe was confused. His life grid seemed to be missing a significant piece, and he had no idea how to solve the puzzle.

Like me, earlier, and perhaps like you, Joe didn't know, but he wanted to know. You are a man. Your life is not working the way you wish it were. You are unfulfilled or others are somehow dissatisfied with you. You ask: "What can I do" or "Why is my life not working?" You need a successful blueprint for your life that works and you need the tools to develop and maintain more satisfying relationships. Read ON!

HOW IS A MAN LIKE A LION?

As a Lion, a man demonstrates the courage to know himself and allow others to know him.

The Lion is willing to be seen and heard, to be curious, and to seek understanding of himself and others. He wants to learn how to express intimacy. He is courageous in his willingness to explore the unknown in order to connect to himself and others.

Life is about knowing and being known. You are designed to know yourself and others. You are hot-wired to experience life so that all of your being is revealed. And yet, this concept scares most of us to death. God designed you to long for someone who understands you, someone with whom to enjoy a relationship. You have an innate desire to know what you like and what you want. You long to sit with another and know that "he or she gets it." When that happens, you come alive. Life works and inspires a creative process from this connection with someone who knows you!

This longing to be known is a reflection of the heart of God to know you and for you to know Him. Jesus prayed in John 17 that all would know "real and eternal life" and he defined that life as KNOWING GOD. The Father desires to be known. He desires to know you, and for that experience to define life as He promised. To be known is the experience of being fully aware of who you are, to be understood completely, to be in deep intimate relationship with another. God wants you to know Him and He wants to know YOU! Listen to the words of Jesus as he prayed for "knowing"....

> Father, it's time.
> Display the bright splendor of your Son
> So the Son in turn may show your bright splendor.
> You put him in charge of everything human
> So he might give real and eternal life to all in his charge.
> And this is the real and eternal life:
> That they know you,
> The one and only true God,

> And Jesus Christ, whom you sent.
> John 17:1-3 (The Message)

Your desire to be known is a healthy kind of narcissism we all possess. You want your thoughts, your ideas, your desires to be understood and appreciated. In a certain sense, somehow it's all about you first and others second. This is not a bad thing; it is a reality of life. Even Jesus used self-love as a measure of our ability to love others when He said in Matthew 22:39: "You shall love your neighbor as yourself."

You can grow beyond narcissism as it is validated. Through the validation of being known and loved by others, you will grow beyond narcissism to empathy. No one can generate love from within themselves. Love from relationship is taken in and metabolized in order to move you from narcissism to empathy, realizing that others exist and you are not the center of the universe. If this process is not available, you will remain stuck in this self-absorbed state. You will then be moved into a place of demand or a place of compliance as you attempt to find your Self.

Developmental growth = move from narcissism to empathy

The Hebrew word "yada" is the word used in the Old Testament to capture this fundamental life principle. "Yada" means to know, to let someone know, to communicate, to inform, and to cause to know. The pattern of Scripture portrays this emotional yearning by God to be known by man, for man to know God, and for people to experience being known by one another.

From the moment of birth to the end of life, the hunger to be known is evident. The baby cries for "Momma" and in so doing is using baby language to say, "I want you to know me, Momma, to know when I am wet, when I am hungry, when I am tired and need sleep. I want to know I can trust you to protect me. I want to know I can depend on you. I want to be cared for." All through life this internal desire to be known and to know is central to experiencing life as the adventure it truly is.

Years ago, I sprained my ankle on a Saturday morning playing basketball with a group of business professionals in Ardmore, Pennsylvania. We should have been playing golf, but our hearts kept telling us we could still play basketball. As I made an "Olympic class" move to the goal in my head, a move that had often freed me for a clear path to the basket as a younger man, my feet failed to get the memo. The result was a rolled left ankle. I could not walk. Some of my friends helped me get to my car and I was able to drive myself to the local community hospital. After sitting in the ER and enduring the customary long wait, I was escorted into a small curtained cubicle. As I sat in my cubicle waiting for the doctor, I experienced a moment I'll never forget. Lying across the hall in another cubicle was a small, white-haired woman. I could see her frail body through the crack in the curtain. She was curled up in the fetal position, crying "Momma…Momma…Momma"! I began to feel the tears well up in my eyes. The lonely, scared cry of this "little one" was no different than what I had heard coming from my infant daughter before I left my house to play basketball. The yearning to know and be known is fundamental to life.

The Lion is committed to the journey of knowing and being known by others. He wants to be real, to experience the joy of relationships, and to be fully alive in the challenge of seeing life as an adventure. He is willing to deal with feeling vulnerable, confused, and frustrated as he becomes more open and engaged. Though it is worth the reward, there is some pain, or at least discomfort, in the process.

Diagram Five shows the Lion in quadrant one. The Bull, Chameleon, and Turtle are evident because you will always have some aspect of each, but the Lion quadrant is ever-expanding. He is always growing in his awareness of Self and in being known by Others.

Being a Lion involves the willingness to be curious, to explore, and to acknowledge. As a Lion, I want to be curious about life in a way that moves me to always learn, always seek, and always hunger for adventure. I then want to explore the deeper aspects of whatever faces me. I want to move into the unfamiliar in a way that stretches me to grow and mature. I want to acknowledge the gifts and talents that I have which help anchor me to the unique person I am. I want to acknowledge the fears and anxieties that seek to rob me of living out the real script that I was designed to live. The Lion is aware!

SELF

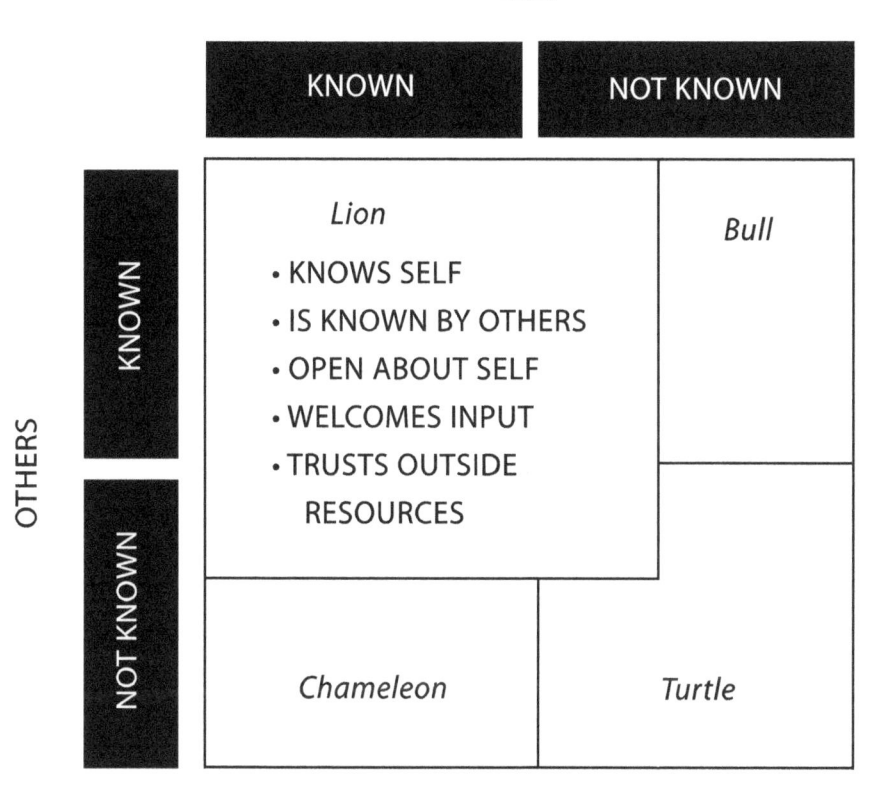

	KNOWN	NOT KNOWN
KNOWN (OTHERS)	*Lion* • KNOWS SELF • IS KNOWN BY OTHERS • OPEN ABOUT SELF • WELCOMES INPUT • TRUSTS OUTSIDE RESOURCES	*Bull*
NOT KNOWN (OTHERS)	*Chameleon*	*Turtle*

DIAGRAM FIVE

Lion = AWARE!

When I checked into the clinic in California that I mentioned in the Prologue, I had no real concept of this paradigm for life. I did not understand that life was more about "yada"—knowing and being known—than it was about doing the right thing or being the right person. I thought I could set goals, learn a new skill, and use discipline to create a better life. I had tried that approach for years, but some of the core concerns of my life were not nurtured or validated by such an approach, leaving these areas unaddressed.

I was ready to learn a new way. The new way was almost immediately confronting me. LIFE IS ABOUT KNOWING. This was the mantra that soon became my guide. The KNOWING was not merely some sort of intellectual exercise. It was all about being connected to the reality that all my problems were relational in some way. I had to learn how to connect myself to others if I was going to live life the way I was designed. I had to be open to being exposed to all that was going on inside me and around me.

Counselors at the clinic quickly told me that if I tried to help someone else there, I would be confronted and asked to be a patient, not a counselor. I was offended and confused. Wasn't this a "helping place?" The answer was obviously YES ... but, I needed to understand that I was the HELPEE, not the HELPER. The very capable staff let me know that I needed to humble myself and receive. I was in need of help and needed to proceed accordingly. As a Group they said to me, over and over, "We want to know you; we want you to be known. Enjoy the process." That scared me to death!

I was uncomfortable, ashamed, and weak. I felt like a complete failure. After all, I was a professional "people helper" and it seemed as if I knew very little about real help. I wanted so much to find life—my life—as it was meant to be experienced. I would work to comply with the directive. I wanted LIFE; besides, I didn't want to get yelled at in Group.

I began telling the story of my life and listening to others react to what they saw and heard in me as I told my story. The staff called this process "feedback." I was surprised by so much that I heard. People laughed at some parts of my story, cried at other parts, and sometimes watched and seemed to hold me as I experienced myself in telling my story.

I was learning to be in touch with myself. I had read hundreds of books about life by this time, but I had never really been fully engaged in the life-giving process of letting others see and experience my good, bad, and ugly parts. It was the difference between reading Swimming for Dummies while sitting poolside versus getting into the water and learning to swim, one small dog paddle at a time. The idea of BEING was in huge contrast to the approach of DOING. I needed to engage ALL of my life. I needed help.

This was the beginning to the second part of understanding LIFE as God designed it to be. Beyond the desire to BE KNOWN is the need to live in COMMUNITY. The reality of being known is only truly found by living in a community, a family of others, who know you, understand you, accept you, and help you see the parts of you that you do not see.

[Sign: Lion = Be known by self and others and live in community]

Jesus expressed a passion for his disciples to live in a community that reflected the intimacy that He had experienced with the Father.

> Father, I want those you gave me
> To be with me, right where I am,
> So they can see my glory, the splendor you gave me,
> Having loved me
> Long before there ever was a world.
> Righteous Father, the world has never known you,
> But I have known you, and these disciples know
> That you sent me in this mission.
> I have made your very being known to them —
> Who you are and what you do —
> And continue to make it known,
> So that your love for me
> Might be in them
> Exactly as I am in them.
> John 17:24-26 (The Message)

In this prayer Jesus reveals His intentional desire for the disciples to experience the intimacy of life that comes from being known and living in community. Jesus is praying that what He has experienced as part of His relationship in the Trinity would be known by His followers. He wants for them what He has with the Father. In contrast to Jesus' desire for an intimate relationship with and for His disciples are His words as He confronts those who say they know Him and even do things in His name, but in reality have no understanding of what Jesus means.

> And then I will declare to them,
> "I never knew you;
> Depart from Me,
> You who practice lawlessness."
> Matthew 7:23 (The Message)

Jesus defines life with Him as being known, a relationship of intimacy! Living a life for eternity requires building a structure that is a firm foundation: a life lived in community. The foundation of community means being fully engaged and embraced by a group that is increasing in its knowledge of you. And as a result, the group is willing to love you with great expressions of acceptance and grace. The community will affirm and validate, as well as offer feedback that may provide guidance and bring you wisdom. Pursuing the life that God designed for you and that He offers you requires that you live a life that is committed to being known in community. Paul gives that instruction to those he was mentoring.

> Now I'm turning you over to God,
> our marvelous God
> whose gracious Word can make you into what he wants you to be
> and give you everything you could possibly need
> in this community of holy friends.
> Acts 20:32 (The Message)

At the clinic, I was learning to be the Lion. I was learning what it means to be real. I was becoming known to a group of other hurting people, all normal in their gifts and weaknesses, all professionals and capable in so many ways. Life for each had come to some kind of abrupt stop, and now they were in this place with me. No one cared what I had done before I arrived, who I was in my profession, or how I could help them now. In fact, to engage with any of that kind of talk would earn me a reprimand from those who were committed to my becoming REAL. I hated the process and yet loved the results I was beginning to see.

BE THE LION: KNOW SELF

What do you like? What do you want? Those questions are fundamental to knowing who you are. You have undoubtedly asked the question "Who am I?" at some time in your life. The answer to that question can only truly come from your heart, and yet most of us live in our head. The answer to "Who am I?" becomes some sort of job description, some functional aspect of your day-to-day existence, or some demand for which you feel responsible. But, putting first things first, your likes and your desires will tell you who you are if you will listen to them.

Several years ago, Linda came to see me with such a question. As I typically do, I escorted her from the waiting area to my office. I left her to settle in as I went to get the paperwork I needed to open her file. When I returned to my office, before I could sit down, she announced, "I am not here to work on my marriage!" I was immediately attuned to her determination to stay in touch with what she had NOT come to get. She was focused and she was letting me know it! I said, "Great! What would you like me to help you with?"

As I took my seat and looked at her, she looked back at me with sad eyes and with a soft tone answered me. She said, "I've been married 35 years; I have raised five boys. They are grown and I am alone with Frank. I have allowed him to have his way so much that the boys have no relationship with him; they do not want to be in the same room with him. I have tried to keep things working between us and between Frank and the boys so much that I've lost myself. I don't know who I am. I don't even know what kind of ice cream I like. I know what Frank likes, but I do not know what I like. I am here to work on me, to find me. I have lost myself. I do not know who I am."

Wow! What a beginning! She was actually further along in the healing process than she realized. She had identified the problem and she knew where she wanted to go. She just did not know how to get there. I said, "I think I can help you!"

The willingness to pursue the knowing of Self is an acknowledgement of how God has made you. You are a needy person … everyone is! Knowing yourself requires you to be honest about feelings, needs, and desires that God wants to meet in you and how the expression of those needs reveals your hunger for God. Knowing Self transports you to a place of need and as you arrive in that vulnerable place, God is waiting to welcome you to His great provision of healing. David modeled that vulnerability:

Knowing yourself = requires honesty about what you want!

> Search me, O God, and know my heart;
> Try me and know my anxious thoughts;
> And see if there be any hurtful way in me,
> And lead me in the everlasting way.
>
> Psalm 139:23-24

BE THE LION: BE KNOWN BY OTHERS

Being known by others is essential to knowing who you are. You have blind spots, parts of you that others see but you do not see. Therefore, you need others involved in your life who will help you know parts of yourself that are true about you, but of which you are unaware (see Diagram One). A blind spot is something that others see about you, but you do not know about yourself. It's like snoring. The one who snores keeps the whole family awake, but he can't figure out why everyone is sitting at the breakfast table looking hung over while he is rested and celebrating the good night's rest he got.

The challenge of being known by others is the risk of being vulnerable and exposed to possible rejection or ridicule. "How can I let you know the parts of me that I am so ashamed of?" Most men do everything possible to hide the illegitimate forms of comfort that shame them, e.g. pornography, addictions, or failures of any sort. A man will never find healing while standing in the darkness of his own attempt to create life. Life is only found in relationship. Isolation kills. A man must be exposed to the parts of himself that others see, but he does not see.

As an example, Bob came to the Men's Coaching Weekend with his anxiety level high. The Coaching Weekend is a weekend experience for men learning to live relationally and in community. Each man is offered the opportunity to share his story. He can tell anything he wants to tell about himself. Bob knew that if he was going to overcome his addiction to pornography he was going to have to stop hiding this broken part of himself. He came to the Weekend knowing that he would have the opportunity to begin healing and overcoming his addiction if he shared this shameful part of his story.

Bob began sharing his life. He told about his family, his career, and his love for sports. Then Bob became silent. I knew Bob was in a struggle within himself. I was sure the voice inside his head was saying, Can I tell this Group about my addiction? What will they do? I feel like such a sleaze ball." Bob was in a war within his own soul. I prayed silently for Bob, knowing that he was fighting for his life. If he shared the secret with the Group, healing could begin, but the fear within Bob told him that he would be in some way rejected.

After much delay, Bob opened his mouth and began telling the Group of his 10-year addiction to pornography, the numerous Internet relations he had with women he had never met, and the comfort he consistently pursued by looking at pictures of women. Watching and listening to Bob was painful as he agonized to form words to describe this shameful, hated part of himself. When Bob finished, every man in the Group could identify with Bob in some way. No one spoke, no one moved. Bob sat with his head down.

I spoke to him. "Bob, what would happen inside of you if we all got up and left the room right now?" Bob said, "My fears would be validated. That's exactly what I would expect you to do." I went over to Bob and knelt down in front of him and said, "Bob, I want you to look at the men in this Group right now. I want you to see in their eyes a picture of yourself. I want you to see what they see, not what you fear they see. Okay? No one is moving. No one is going to leave. Every man here can identify with your story. We may not share in your addiction, but we understand the shame you feel, the effort you have made to stop and the repeated failure you have experienced. We are not going anywhere! Bob, tell me what you see."

> Fully known = knowing the good and bad parts of Self!

Bob reluctantly looked up and scanned the group of men who were focused on him. I asked Bob what he saw. Bob began weeping. "I see understanding and acceptance, compassion and care." I said, "Bob, these men care about you, they care about your story, they see you in a way that you do not see yourself. I want you to take into your soul what you are seeing in their eyes because what you see in their eyes is more true about you than what you believe about you." Bob was beginning to allow himself to be known by others. He was beginning the healing process of overcoming his addiction.

Being known by others requires a commitment to living

relationally, living in community. To be fully known, you must know your good, healthy traits and characteristics and you must know the bad, broken aspects of yourself. Often, you will offer your good parts to others, while doing all you can to hide the bad parts. When that happens you create a split that invites comfort from unhealthy sources like addictions and other behaviors that produce shame and guilt. Only when you can offer your good parts AND your bad parts into a safe community do you grow, heal, and become the man you are designed to be.

Only when you allow yourself to be known by others do you begin to live as a Lion. You must be known by the Group; you must live in community. James says it well:

> Real wisdom, God's wisdom,
> begins with a holy life and is characterized by getting along with others.
> It is gentle and reasonable, overflowing with mercy and blessings,
> not hot one day and cold the next, not two-faced.
> You can develop a healthy, robust community that lives right with God
> and enjoy its results only if you do the hard work of getting along with each
> other, treating each other with dignity and honor.
> James 3:17 (The Message)

BE THE LION: KNOW OTHERS

"I really want to know what makes you tick." Those words may be irresistible and draw the hearer to the sender. Or, it may be frightening and cause the hearer to withdraw or avoid. When you say those words you are letting the other person know that you are willing to pursue them. You have placed the focus on the other person and you are communicating that you want to get to know him or her; you want a relationship. You have targeted the person. You desire to know him or her. This is the way of the Lion.

Knowing others is a risky and vulnerable act. When you enter into this adventure you may be rejected, you will undoubtedly be confronted by a different view of the world, and you may be exposed to parts of yourself that are unknown to you. Knowing others will stretch you and call you out of your own narrow view of them and stretch you. You will be called to accept differences and enlarge your view of life in ways that are seemingly impossible. The pursuit of knowing another is a movement toward personal freedom—freedom from selfishness, fear, and isolation within you.

> *Knowing others = freedom from selfishness, fear, and isolation*

You will grow as you open yourself to others' view of the world and life. This movement to see others' view is a normal and necessary part of developmental growth. Paul calls for being fully engaged with all those that God brings our way.

> Bless those who persecute you;
> Bless and curse not.
> Rejoice with those who rejoice,
> And weep with those who weep.
> Be of the same mind toward one another;
> Do not be haughty in mind,
> But associate with the lowly.
> Do not be wise in your own estimation.
> Romans 12:14-16

As I write this, I am sitting in a coffee shop reflecting on my marriage. I'm struck by how different my wife is from me. She is logical, rational, and assertive. I am feeling-oriented, people-focused, and a pleaser. She is more like the "prototypical man" in our relationship. I am more like the "prototypical woman" in our marriage.

3 critical tools for knowing others = 1) mystery 2) curiosity 3) adventure

As I drink my second cup, I reflect on the interesting dance in our relationship. She is what we call in family therapy circles the "distancer" and I am the "pursuer." She is generally more distant in the relationship as a way to protect herself, and I am generally wanting more contact to soothe my anxiety. Today is one of those days I'm acutely aware of that dance. When I reach this point, I generally become angry, discouraged, and depressed. I feel hopeless and helpless.

I learned that the antidote for this crazy dance is to find the desire to really understand my wife, the sincere desire to know her. This requires working with three critical pieces of reality: mystery, curiosity, and adventure. When I choose to pick up these three tools like a pick, a hoe, and a shovel I begin to dig into the heart of my wife in a way that brings healing to me, to her, and to our relationship. These three tools begin replacing the blame, criticism, and anger that so easily imprison me in my own self-pity or destructive belly-aching.

These tools are at the core of what it means to know others. I want to explore, to be curious, and to work with the mystery of the uniqueness of another human being. Seeing another person for who he or she is in all his or her glory and brokenness is a redemptive process for me. As I sit with my wife in a time of personal frustration in our relationship and pursue her with the primary motivation of just knowing her: "I want to know how you tick," I am freed from the bondage of my own criticism. Judgment is removed and I am able to see her as she truly is.

Knowing others = frees you from blame and criticism

Knowing others is a selfless and deliberate act, an intentional act to humble yourself before another. The act is a weapon against YOUR need to be right. Knowing others is an assertive step of maturity that moves you away from "I'm right and you're wrong" thinking to a place of valuing the relationship more than justifying your own position. You move into a new modality of solving frustration and anxiety by a willingness to sit with another and listen. "I want to know how you tick" is a humbling place to sit when every fiber of your being cries out to dance that crazy, familiar dance of blame and criticism.

I call this the "Kumbaya Thing." Most everyone has been at summer camp or some sort of gathering where the song "Kumbaya" is sung around a fire. The "Kumbaya Thing" is the idea of simply sitting with another. Don't go cut sticks, don't roast marshmallows, and don't go gather more firewood. Simply sit with the other person in order to know, to experience, and to understand him or her. The experience of sitting with another person can be so uncomfortable that many find it impossible. The "Kumbaya Thing" is a totally foreign and frightening concept for most men.

Scary = simply sitting with another person!

The tool of mystery is an acknowledgment that "I don't know, but

I am willing to explore the unknown puzzle by observing, listening, and attuning myself to the music of another." I slow down, sit before you, and let you know that I do not know how to love well, but I am willing to learn. In other words, "Teach me how to love you; I want to know you! I will work with mystery as a way of knowing you!"

The state of curiosity is a step into humility that comes from asserting the personal desire to understand another. It says, "I see you as someone to understand," as opposed to "I see you as something to fix or solve," and "I want to know how you operate and how you experience life." Curiosity is an even greater position of knowing the mystery because curiosity invites open revealing without judgment. Phrases like "tell me more" and "help me understand" replace phrases like "why did you do that?" and/or "you make me angry." Curiosity invites you to reveal yourself to me and prevents me from being judgmental.

The experience of adventure invites me to walk with you as we journey together. I see you as a companion on a trip into the unknown, a reason to be excited about seeing new and different things. I expect you to be different. I no longer want to "fix" you, but rather learn from you and enter your world that is so different from mine. I want to enjoy you the way I would enjoy the whitewater of the Colorado River. I would never want to remove the whitewater. It's what makes the river so attractive to those who look for adventure. It can be very scary, and it can be very exciting. But, I must learn to go with it and not fight against its power. Enjoy the adventure!

Knowing others requires you to sacrifice yourself in order to gift another with the experience of really being known. You are called to be a KNOWER. You are invited to know others. It is the way of the Lion, as the apostle Paul points out here:

> If you've gotten anything at all out of following Christ,
> If His love has made any difference in your life,
> If being in a community of the Spirit means anything to you,
> If you have a heart,
> If you care—
> Then do me a favor:
> Agree with each other,
> Love each other,
> Be deep-spirited friends.

> Don't push your way to the front;
> Don't sweet-talk your way to the top.
> Put yourself aside, and help others get ahead.
> Don't be obsessed with getting your own advantage.
> Forget yourselves long enough to lend a helping hand.
> Philippians 2:1-4 (The Message)

BE THE LION: KNOW THE REAL YOU

You are designed to function as a whole person. The Real You is the YOU with both acceptable traits and hidden defenses. Your defenses are the inhibitions and prohibitions that keep you from connecting to those you love and those who love you. Your Real Self happens when you are free to express both the good, working, functional parts of yourself and the bad, broken, dysfunctional parts of yourself. Both your good parts and your bad parts need love in order for you to become the Real You. Honesty is required.

Becoming the Lion is a personal journey of growth and development. You are asked to work with what "is" in order to overcome the defenses and strategies that you have used to survive the less-than-perfect experiences of life. Your Real self has been lost in a broken world and will be realized only as you face the wounds and the resulting maladaptive defenses that were constructed in you for survival. You do all you can to hide the parts of you that are broken and do not function as they were designed. You may even begin to hate the parts of you that seem to be less acceptable to those around you. They possibly even reflect your weakness and brokenness in the form of criticism toward you.

Real = acknowledge BOTH parts: broken and unbroken

Acknowledging both the unbroken parts and broken parts of yourself is the pathway to seeing life as it IS and thus becoming a fully integrated and highly functioning self. What is IS! The promise of life is that the truth will set you free. Jesus promised it!

> If you stick with this,
> Living out what I tell you,
> You are my disciples for sure.

> Then you will experience for yourselves the truth,
> And the truth will set you free.
> John 8:31-32 (The Message)

As you look at the aspects of yourself that are good, those character traits that truly help you to connect with others, an exciting part of your Real Self comes into focus. However, you also must acknowledge the qualities that keep you from relationship. Talking about, putting words to, or telling the story of the experiences that moved you to hide parts of your personality is when healing begins as you get those parts loved in a group. However, denying behaviors that alienate or hinder relationship will keep you from the growth and healing that could be yours. You will never see the Real You unless you begin the process of putting words to the pain that has caused you to become protective, to hide, and to see survival as your primary motivation.

Real you = put words to pain!

Life seems to compel you to offer what you think (rightly or wrongly!) are your good parts to others and to hide the parts of you that do not work as well. Succumbing to that strategy leaves you with aspects of your personality that are unloved and frozen in a place of denial. You are YOU, which means that you have good parts of you that allow you to connect to God and others, and you have parts that keep you from relationship with God and others. You must own ALL those parts and offer them into loving relationships in order to grow and heal.

This discipline is an exercise toward freedom. You will find healing and completeness as you increase in your honesty about what is going on inside you. The Bible makes this point plainly:

> Make this your common practice:
> Confess your sins to each other and pray for each other
> So that you can live together whole and healed.
> The prayer of a person living right with God
> is something powerful to be reckoned with.
> James 5:16 (The Message)

The freedom in acknowledging the effects of sin upon my life is powerful. Confession is not just about acknowledging what I have done wrong, but also acknowledging how wrong has been done against me.

The Real You is best understood in the idea of BOTH. One part of you is the acceptable parts, your strengths, what you like about yourself and what others like about you. Then, there is the part of you that you do not like to admit exists, those aspects of you that you do not like, the characteristics that may seem unacceptable or unwanted. The reality is that you are BOTH. Even Solomon understood the reality and freedom in acknowledging BOTH.

> I've seen it all in my brief and pointless life—
> Here a good person cut down in the middle of doing good,
> There a bad person living a long life of sheer evil.
> So don't knock yourself out being good,
> And don't go overboard being wise.
> Believe me, you won't get anything out of it.
> But don't press your luck by being bad, either.
> And don't be reckless.
> Why die needlessly?
> It's best to stay in touch with both sides of an issue.
> A person who fears God deals responsibly with all of reality,
> Not just a piece of it.
> Ecclesiastes 7:16-18 (The Message)

Solomon understood the need to see both good and bad as part of reality. This acknowledgement is the acceptance of reality without trying to place quantitative right or wrong to behavior, or to take a moral position on behavior, or to be so concerned with the role of obedience that you cannot simply admit the experience without fear of rejection or hiding from your own shame. This discipline requires a relational paradigm of life versus a paradigm of law that is most concerned with "what is right" or "what is wrong." A relational paradigm moves you to accept, acknowledge, and respect others before casting a judgment of "right" or "wrong." Jesus knows that without grace first, a safe place of acceptance, we have no hope of growing into the man He designed us to be.

With the arrival of Jesus, the Messiah, that confusing dilemma is resolved.

> Those who enter into Christ's being-here-for-us
> no longer have to live under a continuous, low-lying black cloud.
> A new power is in operation.
> The Spirit of life in Christ, like a strong wind,
> Has magnificently cleared the air, freeing you
> From a lifetime of brutal tyranny at the hands of sin and death.
> Romans 8:1-2 (The Message)

Healing = uncover what is broken!

Jesus knows unless you have a place of grace, safety, understanding, and forgiveness, you will only try to cover your faults. God wants you to be known, to reveal, to acknowledge our lives before Him. Remember: what you cover, God will uncover. What God uncovers, He heals.

The Real You is the truth of being created in His image, the intrinsic worth of being human, all that is good about you. And yet, parts of you are broken and less than perfect. To deny either one of those realities and to live without a growing awareness of both your acceptable parts that do work and your unacceptable or flawed parts that do not work will leave you in isolation. The Real You can only be experienced in the light of loving, accepting relationship that overcomes the darkness of alienation. Such integration takes intention and effort.

Let me seek to clarify this truth through a basketball story. I played basketball through high school and college and have many great memories of the good times of competition, of being on a team, and of improving my skills as a basketball player. I am right-handed. I can never remember a time when I could not dribble a basketball with my right hand. It seems that I practically came out of my mother's womb dribbling a basketball with my right hand. My right hand was my strength.

I can remember when I was in the fourth grade becoming very conscious of my inability to dribble the basketball with my left hand. I was confronted with my weakness. I was very aware of how the coach challenged the players to work on the weak parts of their game. I began to practice dribbling with my left hand. For hours I worked to get my spastic left hand to cooperate and be fully integrated with my right hand. By the time I reached high school, I could dribble well with either hand. The right hand was naturally strong, and the left took intentional work.

The Real You is the acknowledgment and acceptance that you have "right-handed" parts of yourself and that you have "left-handed" parts of yourself. If you offer only your "right-handed" parts to the world, then you will never be real. Through the journey of personal growth that strengthens and brings your "left-handed" parts into a place of love and acceptance, you become fully integrated. You become the Real You. YOU BECOME THE LION.

You must be willing to grow and to practice...practice...practice!

> I have a lot more to say about this,
> But it is hard to get it across to you
> since you've picked up this bad habit of not listening.
> By this time you ought to be teachers yourselves,
> Yet here I find you need someone to sit down with you
> And go over the basics on God again,
> Starting from square one—
> Baby's milk,
> When you should have been on solid food long ago!
> Milk is for beginners,
> Inexperienced in God's ways;
> Solid food is for the mature,
> Who have some practice in telling right from wrong.
> Hebrews 5:11-14 (The Message)

WHAT DOES A LION WANT?

Above all, the Lion values being known by self and others. He is committed to a relational approach to life. He wants to be connected to every aspect of himself — to the thinking, feeling, acting, and sensing parts of himself, as well as to those around him. The Lion is active and courageous in the pursuit of whatever will bring him into close, intimate relationship with God and others. The Lion's roar is a call for relationship!

Lion's roar = call for relationship!

As I write this I have just left a group of men who have all participated at some point in a Men's Coaching Weekend. These men are clear on their desire to be the Lion. They are all aware of how broken and weak they are in so many ways. Please understand that if YOU met any of these men YOU would be meeting men from a wide-range of abilities and skills. The group is made up of doctors, entrepreneurs, painters, truck drivers, school teachers, and professionals from all sorts of backgrounds. And yet, what the men offer to one another is a safe and supportive place where they can speak openly about their brokenness. These men are committed to growing by sharing honestly the areas of their lives that could be easily hidden if not for the safe place the Group offers them. These men want to be Lions! The men understand the powerful expression of David as he honestly acknowledges his internal world.

> Count yourself lucky, How happy you must be—
> You get a fresh start,
> Your slate's wiped clean.
> Count yourself lucky—
> God holds nothing against you
> And you're holding nothing back from him.
> When I kept it all inside,
> My bones turned to powder,
> My words became daylong groans.
> The pressure never let up;
> All the juices of my life dried up.
> Then I let it all out;
> I said, "I'll make a clean breast of my failures to God."
> Suddenly the pressure was gone—
> My guilt dissolved,
> My sin disappeared.
> These things add up. Every one of us needs to pray;
> When all hell breaks loose and the dam bursts
> We'll be on high ground, untouched.
> God's my island hideaway,
> Keeps danger far from the shore,
> Throws garlands of hosannas around my neck.
> Let me give you some good advice;
> I'm looking you in the eye
> And giving it to you straight:
> "Don't be ornery like a horse or mule
> That needs bit and bridle to stay on track."
> God-defiers are always in trouble:
> God-affirmers find themselves loved
> Every time they turn around.
> Celebrate God.
> Sing together—everyone!

All you honest hearts, raise the roof!
Psalm 32 (The Message)

These men believe in the power of honesty and the freedom found in Christ to openly express their hearts honestly. You can experience that! The Lion is committed to the pursuit of growing in his ability to know and be known. He wants relationship and connection. He wants the freedom to offer himself without restraint in both his strength and his weakness. He wants to accept and support YOU, in both your gifts and flaws.

WHAT DOES A LION FEAR?

Isolation kills!

The Lion fears the loss or alienation of relationship. He is most disturbed when hurt, fear, and defensiveness prevent him from sharing himself or being open with you. The Lion knows the deadly nature of isolation. He knows that to be truly alone and unknown is the greatest enemy. To have no one to share a sunset, a birthday, or a loss with is to truly experience death.

The Lion knows that secrets provide the darkness where guilt and shame can grow like mold in an unlighted shower—the more darkness, the more mold. Hiding, avoidance, and denial create callousness in a man's heart that prevents the real feeling necessary to form healthy, intimate relationships. He knows he must put words to his experience, whatever that might be. To be expressive is to be alive! To be silent is a march into separation from those he loves and who love him. The Lion searches for buried places within himself and his relationships so he can expose what is hidden to the light of relationship.

To be expressive is to be ALIVE!

In Ephesians the apostle Paul addresses the need to bring light into dark places and to be committed to NOT keeping secrets.

> Don't let yourselves get taken in by religious smooth talk.
> God gets furious with people who are full of religious sales talk
> But want nothing to do with him.
> Don't even hang around people like that.
> You groped your way through that murk once,
> But no longer.
> You're out in the open now.
> The bright light of Christ makes your way plain,
> So no more stumbling around.
> Get on with it!
> The good, the right, the true—
> These are the actions appropriate for daylight hours.
> Figure out what will please Christ,
> And then do it.
> Don't waste your time on useless work, mere busywork,
> The barren pursuits of darkness.
> Expose these things for the sham they are.
> It's a scandal when people waste their lives on things they must do
> in the darkness
> Where no one will see.
> Rip the cover off those frauds and see how attractive they look in
> the light of Christ.
> Ephesians 5:7-13 (The Message)

Paul was clear in his challenge to honest living. A more literal rendering of verse 12 is a description of those who choose to live with secrets.

> For it is disgraceful even to speak of the things
> Which are done by them in secret.
> Ephesians 5:12

Expose and grow!

When a man tells his story I often ask him, "Have you ever told that to anyone before?" The question is often met with a bewildered look and then a big "NO," with the implicit message being "why would I want to do that?" Only when a man overcomes the fear of exposure can he expect to experience the richness of maturity that he seeks.

The Lion fears that some part of his life is hidden, even from himself. He fears that he will not be all that he is designed to be because he has not discovered that hidden part of himself that has held him back. Fear says "hide!" The Lion roars to be heard and seen! He fully embraces and understands the healing effect of the words from First John:

> *The roar of the Lion = Hear me! See me! Know me!*

If we claim that we're free of sin,
We're only fooling ourselves.
A claim like that is errant nonsense.
On the other hand, if we admit our sins—
Make a clean breast of them—
He won't let us down;
He'll be true to himself.
He'll forgive our sins and purge us of all wrongdoing.
If we claim that we've never sinned,
We out-and-out contradict God— make a liar of him.
A claim like that only shows off our ignorance of God.
1 John 1:9-10 (The Message)

WHAT IS IT LIKE TO BE WITH A LION?

When you are with a Lion you have the experience of being WELCOMED! It's like a personal representation of the mat that so many of us have at our front door. The message is, "I AM GLAD YOU ARE HERE!" There is an energy that seems to take hold of you and escort you into a warm, friendly environment. YOU ARE HOME!

There are no fears, no pretensions, and no hidden agenda. There is an ease to sitting with a Lion. He reveals himself just enough so you feel invited into relationship with him. There is no emotional poker playing, i.e. hiding "cards" that make you unsure of where you stand. He evokes in you a relaxed openness that allows you to drop defenses. He asks few questions, but rather chooses to use self-disclosure to invite conversation. There is mutual sharing as opposed to being dominated by too much information about him or too much fact gathering from you.

To be with a Lion = to be with greatness!

When you are with a Lion you are with greatness without feeling "less than." His greatness is his invitation for YOU to be fully YOU. The Lion is glad to have you present, just as you are. You never feel judged or condemned. The Lion looks you in the eyes when he talks to you and does the same when he listens to you. The Lion offers you a safe and secure relationship in which you can be heard and understood. He makes you better by offering himself to you. The experience is simultaneously powerful and safe.

David offers a picture of a Lion as he describes a man in whom the grace of God is at work.

> How blessed is the man who fears the Lord,
> Who greatly delights in His commandments.
> His descendants will be mighty on earth;
> The generation of the upright will be blessed.
> Wealth and riches are in his house,
> And his righteousness endures forever.
> Light arises in the darkness for the upright;
> He is gracious and compassionate and righteous.
> It is well with the man who is gracious and lends;
> He will maintain his cause in judgment.
> For he will never be shaken;
> The righteous will be remembered forever.
> He will not fear evil tidings;
> His heart is steadfast, trusting in the Lord.
> His heart is upheld, he will not fear,
> Until he looks with satisfaction on his adversaries.
> He has given freely to the poor;
> His righteousness endures forever;
> His horn will be exalted in honor.
> The wicked will see it and be vexed;
> He will gnash his teeth and melt away;
> The desire of the wicked will perish.
> Psalm 112

This is a Hebrew acrostic psalm that describes a godly man. The psalm follows the Hebrew alphabet in order to describe a godly man, a Lion! Who wouldn't want to be with a Lion?

WHAT MAKES A LION A LION?

A Lion is courageous! A Lion does three things really well. He reveals, he receives, and he trusts. A man who exercises these three actions will be engaged in the life he was designed to enjoy.

1. A LION REVEALS.

A Lion reveals who he is. He offers himself freely and completely to others. The Lion is aware of his strength and his power, but he does not use it destructively. He is not afraid of his weakness or inability to be perfect. To the Lion, life is not about being right or wrong or perfect, but about being connected to himself and to those he loves. He values honest self-disclosure as a means to be real and be part of the human race. The Lion is not afraid to expose who he really is—in all his power and beauty—and in all his faults and failures. He is not about hiding, but revealing. And in that way, he is truly courageous!

As the true Man, Jesus' purpose was to reveal. He revealed Himself and, in so doing, revealed God, the Father. Jesus taught the importance of all things becoming known as a means of discipleship.

> For the time is coming when everything will be revealed;
> All that is secret will be made public.
> Matthew 10:26 (New Living Translation)

The importance of making known what is unknown is central to the message and person of Jesus.

> Those who obey my commandments are the ones who love me.
> And because they love me, my Father will love them,
> And I will love them.
> And I will reveal myself to each one of them.
> John 14:21 (New Living Translation)

The man who begins to reveal himself in order to develop relationship and connection is the man who is willing to embrace vulnerability and humility as means to life. Genuine revealing is not a narcissistic ploy to proclaim one's right or demand, but an honest expression of the heart. I love the movie Life As a House. Actor Kevin Kline plays a character named George who lives in a run-down house that symbolizes his sad life. After a heart attack, being fired from his job of 20 years, and being diagnosed with cancer and being given 4 months to live, he chooses to re-build his house and thus begin the process of re-building his life.

As his ex-wife drives him home from the hospital, George reveals his desire to take his son for the summer in order to re-build their relationship. He wants to re-build his house, re-build his broken relationship with his son, and begin the process of re-building his life. George takes a stand to begin living from his heart and that overt step is the revealing of what he truly wants. He chooses to reveal, rather than live in denial of what is most deeply true of him, and become a Lion.

Life = embrace vulnerability and humility!

When a man begins to reveal his true desires, he begins to live as he was meant to live, to live from his heart. He is neither demanding nor defensive. I recently sat with a man named Brad as he revealed his heart to me. He said, "I am so sorry for how I have wasted so many opportunities in my life to love and to grow. I have been selfish and narcissistic. I want a second chance … I feel so broken … I'm scared." Brad's wife had recently moved out after years of trying to get Brad to listen to her. She had tried many times to let him know how demanding and angry he was toward her and their children. She had lost hope and tolerance. Now Brad was living in the big house alone, praying he could restore what was now so broken. I knew his best chance was to begin learning how to reveal himself to his wife, rather than attempting to manage or control her.

Reveal versus manage or control

A man is a Lion as he reveals himself. He reflects the character of God in the way that God acts to reveal Himself to mankind. He makes himself known! Hear the words of Jesus as he reflects this idea to Peter:

> Jesus replied, "You are blessed, Simon son of John,
> Because my Father in heaven has revealed this to you.
> You did not learn this from any human being.
> John 16:17 (New Living Translation)

2. A LION RECEIVES.

The importance of being able to receive is a fundamental tenant to experiencing God and embracing life. The Gospel of John reveals how important being able to receive truly is. Unless you learn to receive, you will not even be integrated into the family of God!

> But as many as received Him,
> To them He gave the right to become children of God,
> Even to those who believe in His name,
> Who were born not of blood,
> Nor of the will of the flesh,
> Nor of the will of man,
> But of God.
> John 1:12-13

The Lion knows how to receive. This is a hard place for most men to sit. The saying, "it is better to give than to receive," is false! Most anyone can give, but to be able to receive is to be placed in a position of humility. Men do not naturally like sitting in such a chair. It is hard to receive, but a man who is committed to growing must be willing to receive feedback from those who see him in ways that he cannot see himself. He is willing to receive support, help, and guidance. To be willing to receive is to be willing to stop the car and ask for directions when lost. OUCH! Most men say, "NO WAY!"

I think of how hard it was for so many men on the Gulf Coast to cope with the realities of Hurricane Katrina. On Sunday, August 28, 2005, many men were in the giving position. They were able to give assistance and support to neighbors. But, by Tuesday morning, August 30, many of those same men had nothing to give. They were forced into a position of receiving. They had lost everything. Someone was now handing them a cup and plate and telling them where to sit and eat. They were humiliated.

A man must receive from God before life begins. No one can self-generate anything that can bring real life. He is humbled in his inability to bring life by his own power. Thus, he is invited into being by receiving what another has to offer him. Only God can give life. By receiving graciously, a man acknowledges his neediness for outside help. That reality started at birth and continues throughout the journey of his life span.

The critical principle of receiving is throughout Scripture. Listen to the words of John the Baptist:

> John answered and said,
> "A man can receive nothing,
> unless it has been given him from heaven."
> John 3:27

Listen as Jesus challenges the Pharisees for their lack of receiving:

Receive = acknowledge need and welcome help!

> You have your heads in your Bibles constantly
> because you think you'll find eternal life there.
> But you miss the forest for the trees.
> These Scriptures are all about me!
> And here I am,
> standing right before you,
> and you aren't willing
> to receive from me the life you say you want.
> John 5:39-40 (The Message)

Jesus instructs the disciples to receive the power they need to continue from the Holy Spirit:

> But when the Holy Spirit has come upon you,
> you will receive power and will tell people about me everywhere
> —in Jerusalem, throughout Judea, in Samaria,
> and to the ends of the earth.
> Acts 1:8 (New Living Translation)

Listen to the promise of being sons of God, able to call him Father as we receive ...

> For you have not received a spirit of slavery leading to fear again,
> but you have received a spirit of adoption as sons
> by which we cry out, "Abba! Father!"
> Romans 8:15

Listen to the promise of new life to all those who receive what Jesus offers as a result of His death and resurrection ...

> He died for everyone
> so that those who receive his new life
> will no longer live to please themselves.
> Instead, they will live to please Christ,
> Who died and was raised for them.
> 2 Corinthians 5:15 (New Living Translation)

Listen to the reality that even the knowledge of God comes from our receiving what He reveals and offers ...

> For I neither received it from man,
> nor was I taught it,
> but I received it through a revelation of Jesus Christ.
> Galatians 1:12

Listen to the result of receiving God's promise ...

> But the Scriptures have declared
> that we are all prisoners of sin,
> so the only way to receive God's promise
> is to believe in Jesus Christ.
> Galatians 3:22 (New Living Translation)

Listen to the promise that one day we will receive ALL that has been promised ...

> But we who live by the Spirit
> eagerly wait to receive everything promised to us
> who are right with God through faith.
> Galatians 5:5 (New Living Translation)

Listen to the invitation to keep coming to God for the help we need ...

> So let us come boldly to the throne of our gracious God.
> There we will receive His mercy,
> and we will find grace to help us when we need it.
> Hebrews 4:16 (New Living Translation)

As a reflection of all that God has revealed about Himself and His plan for mankind, a man that is a Lion is committed to receiving as a way to LIFE. The Lion receives willingly. He welcomes input and feedback. He sees it as a gift. He asks for support from a community of friends and wise counselors. The Lion can sit and hear the hard things about how he is bringing hurt to his wife, his family, or his community. He can also receive the acknowledgement of his gifts and abilities to make the world a better place without moving into pride or being inhibited by shame. The Lion is courageous in this way!

Thomas recently sat with his wife as she read from the list she had written on the back of an envelope. She had taken the time to organize her pain, blame, and criticism as his wife in an orderly, objective format. Because she had indicated she was separating from him, he listened for the first time even though they had been married for almost 20 years. She was exhausted from years of his not listening to her. He was now facing the tragedy of losing his marriage because he had been so unwilling to receive her view of him. I felt for him and I felt for her. It is so tragic to see two people who love each other be so alienated and perplexed at how to be WITH each other. I was reminded of Jesus' words when He said, "I never knew you." Receiving is so necessary!

> Truly, truly I say to you,
> he who receives whom ever I send receives Me;
> and he who receives Me receives Him who sent Me.
> John 13:20

The man who is unwilling to receive is truly a man who is lost … lost in every way! The Lion receives!

3. THE LION TRUSTS.

Finally, the Lion knows how to trust. As strong as he is, he still knows how to have a healthy sense of dependency. The words "I need you" or "I know we can" are phrases that he uses freely and confidently because he knows how to trust others. Certainly, when he trusts he opens himself up to the reality of pain that comes when he is failed by the one he trusts. At that point, he is able to work to forgive and to reconcile. He neither demands flawlessness nor expects perfection in others or in himself. He is able to trust because he is a man of character— a man who is known for his integrity, values, and principles. Life is not about his or others' performance or accomplishments. The Lion knows that life is about relationship and that trusting in others is necessary and yet dangerous. The Lion is courageous in this way!

The foundation for trust is rooted in your past experiences. Your ability to trust now depends on how secure and available the people in your background have offered themselves. You will trust well as you have consistent experiences of caretakers who met your needs and presented nurture. But, when you have often experienced disappointment and pain as a result of placing your trust in others, then you will be anxious and distant in your willingness to trust others. Fears, shallow relationships, anger, and addictions will fill a man's life when the level of trust is reduced.

Jesus invited trust. On the occasion when a synagogue official was told his daughter had died, Jesus encouraged him to trust.

Trust = healthy dependence!

> Jesus overheard what they were talking about and said to the leader, "Don't listen to them; just trust me."
> Mark 5:36 (The Message)

On another occasion, Jesus esteemed the trust of a Roman military leader whose slave was sick and about to die. The Roman soldier wanted Jesus' help, but resisted having Jesus trouble Himself by coming to his house. So he sent word that Jesus only needed to give an authoritative command and his slave would be healed. When Jesus heard these words, He responded.

Taken aback, Jesus addressed the accompanying crowd:

> "I've yet to come across this kind of simple trust
> anywhere in Israel,
> the very people who are supposed to know about God and how he works."
> When the messengers got back home, they found the servant up and well.
> Luke 7:9-10 (The Message)

On another occasion, Jesus attempted to comfort those who were being intimidated by Jewish leaders to trust Him. Upon observing those afraid to trust Him, He cried out:

> Jesus shouted to the crowds,
> "If you trust me,
> you are trusting not only me,
> but also God who sent me.
> John 6:44 (The Message)

We are assured that trust is what opens the intervention of God's provision to us! By trust in the King, life is offered in the kingdom of God. Trust is the key!

> *The object of trust > the amount of trust!*

"No one who trusts God like this—heart and soul—
will ever regret it."
It's exactly the same no matter what a person's religious background may be:
the same God for all of us,
acting the same incredibly generous way to everyone who calls out for help.
"Everyone who calls, 'Help, God!' gets help."
Romans 10:11 (The Message)

We are warned to trust in what is trustworthy. The object of your trust is greater than the quantity of your trust. What you trust in MATTERS!

> Instead of trusting in our own strength or wits to get out of it,
> We were forced to trust God totally—not a bad idea
> Since he's the God who raises the dead!
> 2 Corinthians 1:9 (The Message)

The man who is growing as a Lion reveals, receives, and trusts. He is strong and courageous in being open … open to exercising his strength … open to acknowledging his weaknesses … open to receiving from others … open to being humble … open to his need to believe in someone beyond himself. It is dangerous. It is uncomfortable. It requires great courage!

CONCLUSION

> *Being open to the life of the Lion = dangerous and requires courage!*

At the beginning of this chapter, I introduced you to Joe and Sally. Joe came to me to understand why Sally was so disappointed with their marriage. Joe's biggest problem was Sally's dissatisfaction and displeasure with him. He was confused as to what Sally wanted from him.

I don't remember exactly what I shared with Joe. Whatever it was, I don't believe it was very helpful. I think I somehow talked about Joe's feelings, but I never connected with Joe anymore than Joe was connecting with Sally. He tolerated my "psycho-babble" for a few sessions and then stopped coming to my office.

I still see Joe now from time to time. We're still friends. He and Sally have survived and remain married in spite of my inability to really help him address the problem in his marriage.

I wish I had been able to share with Joe what I have addressed in this chapter with you. The idea of being known and knowing another, the process of becoming a Lion, of becoming Real, is what I believe Joe was asking of me. He wanted to understand how to be a man, and how to develop intimacy in his relationships with those he loved. Joe's questions helped me to integrate my own growth with the ability to help another man understand how to experience a more rewarding life.

Since I sat with Joe, I have talked to hundreds of men who have embraced the principles in this book. Men have learned how to sit with their wives, their children, their friends, and breathe in the life that comes only from learning how to relate to God and to the important people in their lives. You can experience that too, if YOU WILL BE COURAGEOUS!

Heed the words of Daniel, and God will do this for YOU!

> "While he was saying all this,
> I looked at the ground and said nothing.
> Then I was surprised by something like a human hand that touched my lips.
> I opened my mouth and started talking to the messenger:
> 'When I saw you, master, I was terror-stricken.
> My knees turned to water. I couldn't move.
> How can I, a lowly servant, speak to you, my master?
> I'm paralyzed. I can hardly breathe!'
> "Then this humanlike figure touched me again and gave me strength.
> He said, 'Don't be afraid, friend. Peace.
> Everything is going to be all right. Take courage. Be strong.'
> "Even as he spoke, courage surged up within me.
> I said, 'Go ahead, let my master speak. You've given me courage.'
> Daniel 10:15-19 (The Message)

Be the LION! Be REAL! Be KNOWN! Be YOU! The Lion was born to ROAR!!!

REMEMBER THIS:

- The Lion demonstrates courage.
- The Lion is courageous in that he is willing to know himself and

be known by others.
- The Lion is willing to be curious, to explore, and to acknowledge.
- The Lion knows that listening to his desires is critical to knowing himself and being in relationship with others.
- The Lion knows that being known by others is essential to knowing self.
- The Lion knows that being known by others requires a commitment to living relationally, living in community.
- The Lion knows that the pursuit of knowing another is a movement toward personal freedom — freedom from selfishness, fear, and isolation.
- The Lion works with mystery, curiosity, and adventure as tools to knowing others.
- The Lion believes that knowing others is a selfless and deliberate act to humble himself and fight against the need to be right.
- The Lion knows that he is Real when he is free to express BOTH the good, working, functional parts of self and the bad, broken, dysfunctional parts of self.
- The Lion values being known by self and by others above all else.
- The Lion knows that to be truly alone and unknown is the greatest enemy.
- The Lion is courageous in his willingness to reveal, receive, and trust.

EPILOGUE: Remember This!

Men's Coaching Weekends offer me the opportunity to sit with Bulls, Chameleons, and Turtles. Occasionally, a Lion even shows up!

David sat with a group of men at his second Men's Coaching Weekend with such a different perspective. When he first attended the Coaching Weekend months before, he was reluctant and anxious. He came as a Chameleon, hiding much of what he knew about himself and fearing that others would see through his camouflaged way of relating. But, now as an alumnus of the weekends, he was a Lion. He sat ready and willing to offer himself to the group and he welcomed the group's feedback to him.

When it came time for David to share, here's a small portion of what he offered to the other men: "This has been the hardest and the best year of my life. In this past year, my marriage came to an end. I am now divorced. The process of the divorce has forced me to see how I failed to love my wife. She tried to get my attention, but I didn't know how to love her. She pleaded with me to love her, to open up to her, and to let her in to my life. I didn't have a clue to what she really was saying to me. On the outside, I was a success to all who thought they knew me. I was respected in the community as a professional, a member of a prominent local church, and had many friends. But, I feared to let anyone really see me up-close, including my wife. I didn't know how to be open, vulnerable, or weak."

"In the midst of my marriage coming to a slow and painful death, I attended my first Deer Camp weekend. The whole experience opened me up to the healing effect of revealing myself to a group of men who accepted me and offered love in areas of my life that I had never shared with anyone. I will never forget listening to music on Sunday morning that opened my heart to God, and for the first time I experienced Him speaking to me personally. I sat with men who opened their life to me, openly acknowledging struggles and failures. The weekend helped me to begin a journey of walking with God, living from my heart, and being in relationship with my children and other men. I have grown so much this year in the midst of the worst year of my life. I am grateful for what I have gone through. I am both happy and sad. I feel so much more connected to my children. I experience God speaking to me through His Word, music, and all sorts of creative ways. I am a different man."

That is the voice of a Lion … the heart of a Lion!

I am so honored to sit with men like David. I love watching God bring the hearts of "dead men" alive. I hurt as they hurt. I rejoice in their victories. I see God doing great things in and through men as they walk through all kinds of tragedies. I believe being in the presence of these men is the experience of being on holy ground. God is at work in the hearts of men. He pursues them like a jilted lover seeking to reclaim the love of his life.

When a man is able to fully acknowledge BOTH his good parts and his bad parts to a community of others, then he is living as a Lion. He is self-aware enough to openly and honestly acknowledge the parts of himself that are broken. He knows he is not able to love the way he wants to love, the way others want him to love, or the way God designed him to love. He owns the parts of him that hurt others. That is not an easy journey. On the other hand, he is aware of the parts of him that bring life to others, how he is able to show care for another, and how he is responsive to a personal relationship with the living God.

He is responsive to the needs of others and is willing to listen to what they offer him regarding his own life. Defensiveness, fear, and anger are swallowed up by the courage to be known. And in that process, a man of rich character is born. Bulls, Chameleons, and Turtles yield to the Lion as he emerges in all his glory!

The final diagram, Diagram Six, shows what is necessary for each of the maladaptive metaphors to move to the Lion quadrant.

Lion = reveals, receives, and risks
Bull = must receive feedback
Chameleon = must reveal hidden parts
Turtle = must risk and trust

Scripture tells us that a man will be known by the fruit he bears. This is a metaphor given by Jesus that helps us know that a man's behavior reveals his character.

SELF

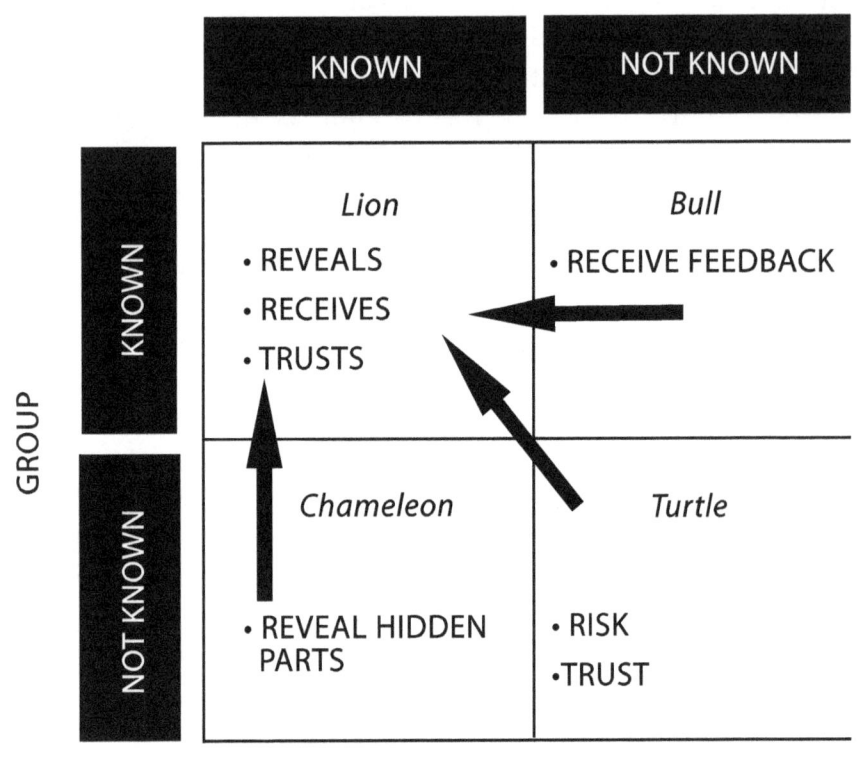

	KNOWN	NOT KNOWN
GROUP — KNOWN	*Lion* • REVEALS • RECEIVES • TRUSTS	*Bull* • RECEIVE FEEDBACK
GROUP — NOT KNOWN	*Chameleon* • REVEAL HIDDEN PARTS	*Turtle* • RISK • TRUST

DIAGRAM SIX

> Every good tree bears good fruit; But the bad tree bears bad fruit.
> So then, you will know them by their fruits.
> Matthew 7:17, 20

Becoming a Lion requires living in relationship. A Bull, a Chameleon, or a Turtle cannot become a Lion unless each commits to living in community. A man's choosing to live in a community that offers safety and acceptance to broken parts that are unknown, hidden, or unconscious will transform him into a Lion. No man can become a Lion unless he is a part of a community. He must be known by others in order to know himself.

By completing this book, you have been exposed to a framework for how life works. It is time for you to begin intentionally seeking to know and be known. You must find a community of men who will help you know yourself. Bulls must be in a place where others can reveal blind spots about you. Chameleons must have a place to reveal parts of your self that you have kept hidden. Turtles must be in relationships that will awaken your unconscious and unaware sleep and move you to new places of risk and force you to trust in resources beyond yourself. In a community of healing, Bulls receive, Chameleons reveal, and Turtles trust. Lions are born in these communities.

I personally am on this journey. I have experienced the pain and the victory of this process. I have come to understand the power of being known. I feel so much freer about my life as I share openly and honestly with men I trust. I am empowered by the support of a community of men who care about me and one another. I see God in all aspects of my life and I experience His presence as real as any relationship I have. He is not distant; He is known and He knows me. My life is about being known and being known is about God. Being a Lion is a spiritual experience of being connected to the living God.

The way of life, the way of the kingdom of God, is to be known. First and foremost is the pursuit of knowing and being known by God Himself. What could be more Lion-like than to be in relationship with the King of the universe! Listen to the words of God as expressed through the prophet Jeremiah:

> Don't let the wise brag of wisdom.
> Don't let heroes brag of their exploits.
> Don't let the rich brag of their riches.
> If you brag, brag of this and this only:
> That you understand and know me.
> I'm God, and I act in loyal love.
> I do what's right and set things right and fair,
> And delight in those who do the same things.
> These are my trademarks. God's Decree.
> Jeremiah 9:23-24 (The Message)

When a man begins to know himself, he sees how broken, inadequate, and needy he truly is. At that point, God offers a healing, forgiving relationship to that man through His Son, Jesus Christ. God does not hand him a "to do" list. He offers him hope for life through the provision made by Jesus Christ. There is no safer place in the entire universe than in the hands of a heavenly Father who has given up His Son to have a relationship WITH YOU! Through the death and resurrection of Jesus Christ, God has offered restoration and healing to you. Take a moment to consider the words from Romans, meditate on them, and hear the voice of God as you read:

> By entering through faith into what God has always wanted to do for us —
> Set us right with Him, make us fit for Him —
> We have it all together with God because of our Master Jesus.
> And that's not all:
> We throw open our doors to God and discover at the same moment that He has already thrown open His door to us.
> We find ourselves standing where we always hoped we might stand—
> Out in the wide open spaces of God's grace and glory,
> Standing tall and shouting our praise.
> There's more to come:
> We continue to shout our praise even when we're hemmed in with troubles,
> Because we know how troubles can develop passionate patience in us,
> And how that patience in turn forges the tempered steel of virtue,
> Keeping us alert for whatever God will do next.
> In alert expectancy such as this, We're never left feeling shortchanged.
> Quite the contrary —
> We can't round up enough containers to hold everything God generously pours into our lives through the Holy Spirit! Christ arrives right on time to make this happen. He didn't, and doesn't, wait for us to get ready. He presented Himself for this sacrificial death when we were far too weak and rebellious to do anything to get ourselves ready. And even if we hadn't been so weak, we wouldn't have known what to do anyway. We can understand someone dying for a person worth dying for, And we can understand how someone good and noble could inspire us to selfless sacrifice. But God put His love on the line for us
> By offering His Son in sacrificial death
> While we were of no use whatever to Him.
> Romans 5:1-8 (The Message)

God REVEALS: HE has REVEALED Himself to you through the person of His Son. God RECEIVES: HE RECEIVES worship because HE is GOD! And only by RECEIVING all that HE has offered through HIS SON, Jesus Christ, can you be restored to the life God designed for you. By TRUSTING in HIM as the object of LIFE, all HIS resources are activated in you to live the LIFE HE promised.

As a reflection of God, a Lion reveals, receives, and trusts. If you follow this pattern, you can be a Lion. However, you will never be a Lion on your own. The task is too great. It's impossible without the resources God provides. But, He offers them to YOU! So YOU choose! GO BE A LION! YOUR ADVENTURE BEGINS NOW!

www.ingramcontent.com/pod-product-compliance
Lightning Source LLC
LaVergne TN
LVHW041920180425
809045LV00001B/87